C000298803

JAPAN

THE W🌐RLD

VEGETARIAN

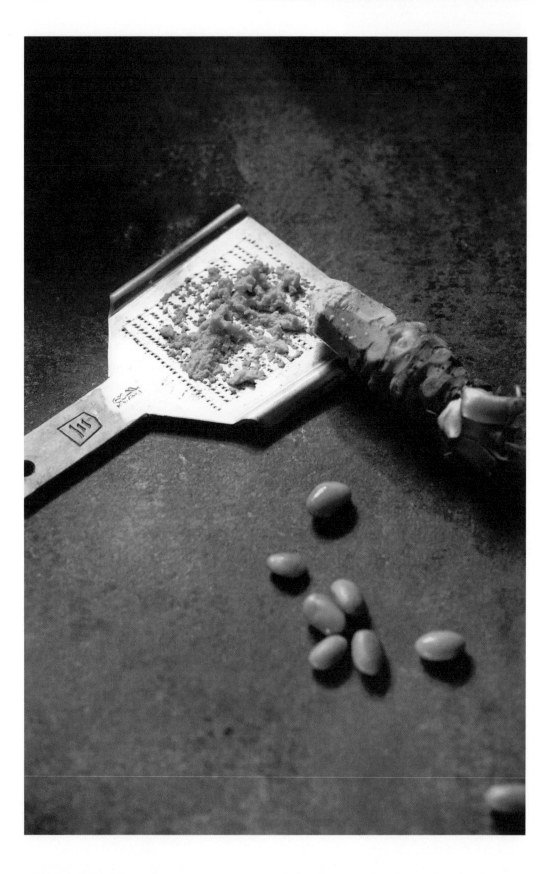

Reiko Hashimoto

JAPAN
THE W🗾RLD
VEGETARIAN

BLOOMSBURY ABSOLUTE

LONDON · OXFORD · NEW YORK · NEW DELHI · SYDNEY

To all the students of Hashi,
with whom I've shared the joys
of Japanese cuisine.

INTRODUCTION

Food is an essential part of Japanese culture. From comforting bowls of ramen or nabe, to beautifully presented sushi, food is everywhere.

The connection between food and the natural environment is clear to see in Japan, as is the connection of ingredients to the season. Stretching back, Japan traditionally produced the food it needed rather than importing goods, and Japanese chefs learnt to cook with the seasons, as well as whatever is available in their specific locality. This tradition is still seen throughout the country, and growing up in Kyoto we always had an abundance of mountain vegetables. Particular favourites of mine include freshly picked bamboo shoots in spring, with their nutty, woody flavour, and the earthy *matsutake* mushroom, also known as the Japanese truffle, which is rampant in autumn.

Japan's landscape is incredibly varied. Consisting of four main islands across 1,900 miles, there are vast mountain ranges which are fertile lands for growing vegetables, rice, mushrooms, fruits and nuts. The climate varies from island to island, and indeed province to province, so each region has its own unique way of preparing what are seen as signature Japanese dishes. For example, *okonomiyaki* in Osaka would be very different from *okonomiyaki* in Hiroshima. Both are a savoury pancake with a base of egg, flour, cabbage and spring onion, to which you can add extra vegetables, but the Osaka version would mix all the extra ingredients in with the base whereas in Hiroshima all the ingredients are layered, with an addition of noodles.

ANCIENT HERITAGE

Kyoto, which happens to be my hometown, is considered to be the Japanese capital for vegetarian food due to its long tradition of *shojin ryori*, the vegan diet eaten by Buddhist monks in Japan. Typically, *shojin ryori* meals are composed of different plant-based foods in a way believed to bring balance and alignment to the body, mind and spirit. Having arrived in the region in the sixth century, *shojin ryori* continues to influence food in Kyoto even today, particularly considering the 'rule of five', whereby each meal offers five colours and five flavours, providing a nutritious, beautiful and delicious dining experience.

Not only home to *shojin ryori*, as a city surrounded by mountains and freshwater springs, Kyoto is also renowned for its tofu, which is a staple of the Japanese diet. It is an incredibly versatile ingredient, high in protein and easy to transform into something delicious. Incidentally it contains less fat and fewer calories than the same quantity of meat. It is one of my favourite ingredients, and the way that it is revered, displayed and enjoyed in Kyoto is similar to cheese in France, with endless varieties available – fresh, aged, firm, soft, creamy, crumbly, fermented, smoked. Within these pages are a number of delicious recipes, encouraging you to embrace this most Japanese of ingredients – I hope you come to love it as I do. (See page 150 for more on tofu.)

BENEFITS OF A JAPANESE DIET

As a health-conscious chef, I have long been aware of the specific health benefits of the Japanese diet. Japan boasts one of the highest life expectancies in the world, and only 3.6 per cent of the Japanese population have a body mass index over 30, which is the international standard for obesity. As a comparison, some other countries have close to a third of the population over this threshold.

The reasons for Japan's favourable statistics are undoubtedly the diet and the fact that many Japanese people subscribe to two notions: that you should eat until you are 80 per cent full, and that you eat with your eyes – a nod to the importance of colours, crockery and food presentation. When we eat with chopsticks, we tend to slow down, and so you find yourself enjoying the sight of your meal for longer.

Typically, Japanese meals consist of an array of textures and flavours. They are eaten slowly and, in comparison to the western diet, contain fewer fats or processed ingredients, and far less dairy and meat. Japan is far from a vegetarian country as we consume a vast amount of fish; however, vegetables and soy products are staple ingredients in our diets, and vegetarianism in Japan is on the rise.

Three of the most common Japanese ingredients are miso, seaweed and tofu. These contain many vitamins and minerals that promote excellent health while, most importantly, leading to mouth-wateringly good food. The fact that they are already essential to a traditional Japanese diet means that the step to vegetarianism is a relatively small one.

As an added bonus, seaweed, an ingredient most associated with Japanese cuisine, is full of calcium and vitamins A and C, all of which are great for your skin, hair and nails. Beyond the exterior benefits, seaweed is known to prevent high blood pressure, promote digestion and aid detoxing. On top of that, it gives a depth of flavour and is a vital ingredient for Japanese vegetarian cooking. (For more see page 94.)

Offering authentic and delicious recipes, this book will give you an insight into the cuisine that gives Japan one of the lowest obesity rates and longest life expectancies in the world. With recipes that have been handed down and slightly adapted across generations, wherever you live, this is a book that will take you to Japan without leaving the comfort of your own kitchen.

STORECUPBOARD INGREDIENTS

Most Japanese kitchens are equipped with these
staple ingredients, and they are vital for creating
authentic Japanese flavours. I'm pleased to say all
of them are easily found in Japanese supermarkets,
some Asian supermarkets and online.

- **Ao-nori (seaweed) powder** A condiment for sprinkling and seasoning, much like
  salt and pepper. *Ao-nori* has the unmistakable flavour of seaweed and is bright green
  in colour (see also page 94).

- **Chilli-infused sesame oil (*rahyu*)** This is often used in Chinese and Japanese dishes
  such as gyoza and ramen.

- **Dried shiitake mushrooms (*hoshi shiitake*)** One of the ingredients for vegetarian
  stock. They have a much stronger flavour than fresh ones and are used in a variety of
  cooked dishes.

- **Japanese horseradish (*wasabi*)** Although this is a type of horseradish, it is somewhat
  different to the Western variety. The root of the horseradish is much smaller and pale
  green in colour. Ready-made pastes or dried forms are widely available, however the
  actual wasabi content present is often extremely low. Fresh wasabi is available online.

- **Japanese mayonnaise (*mayonaizu*)** Japanese mayonnaise is much more yellow
  in colour than the typical Western mayonnaise as it contains more egg yolk. It is also
  creamier and has a more citrussy flavour.

- **Kombu dashi powder (*kombu dashi no moto*)** Dashi stock powder is something
  the Japanese use daily. Instant kombu dashi stock is the vegetarian alternative to the
  fish-based one and likewise available in powder form. Simply stir the powder or liquid
  into boiling water.

- **Konnyaku yam cake** This has very little taste of its own and is perfect to cook slowly
  to absorb all the other flavours. It has a slightly oceanic taste and smell of seaweed. It
  is valued more for its texture than for its flavour and is a good for low-calorie diets as it
  has virtually no calories.

- **Miso** There are many types of this fermented soy bean paste (see more on page 52).
  Miso is mostly used for soups but also for marinades, sauces and salad dressings.
  Miso paste can be kept in an airtight container in the refrigerator for up to one year
  but tends to get saltier as it ages.

- **Noodles**: There are many different varieties, including: dried noodles (*kanmen*); soba – brown buckwheat noodles, the healthiest of all the noodles (you can obtain different flavours such as green tea or yuzu); somen – fine white wheat flour noodles with silky texture; ramen – originally from China, made of wheat flour and eggs; udon – thick, white, wheat flour noodles.

- **Rice vinegar (*komezu*)** Milder than most Western vinegars, it is mainly used for sushi rice, salad dressing and in some simmered dishes. Cider vinegar can be substituted with a little water added.

- **Rice wine (*sake*)** Dry rice wine used for cooking and drinking. Traditionally, sake is enjoyed warm though in recent years it has become popular served cold.

- **Sansho pepper (*sansho*)** The sansho or prickly ash tree also yields fragrant *kinome* leaves, which are often used as a garnish. Earthy, tangy and lemony in flavour, when these leaves are placed directly on your tongue you notice a tingling sensation. *Sansho* is usually sold ground and typically used on grilled foods.

- **Seaweed** See page 94.

- **Sesame oil (*goma abura*)** Toasted sesame seeds are pressed to form an oil that is typically used for flavouring rather than cooking.

- **Seven-spice powder (*shichimi*)** Widely used as a dried condiment, the mixture of seven spices also includes chilli as a dominant ingredient.

- **Short-grain brown rice (*genmai*)** Being the least refined and most nutritious rice, brown rice is high in fibre, but it does take much longer to cook than white rice. It is also chewier and nuttier.

- **Short-grain rice (*gohan*)** Short- or medium-grain rice is most suitable for Japanese dishes. Buy rice made in Japan if possible, but short-grain rice from California, Australia, Spain and Korea is also suitable.

- **Soy sauce (*shoyu*)** A basic ingredient used in most Japanese dishes as it is the salt agent. It is much less salty than Chinese soy sauce. Tamari is another type of Japanese soy sauce and it is gluten free.

- **Sushi vinegar (*sushizu*)** A special blend of rice vinegar, sugar, salt and dashi. A bottle of ready-to-use sushi vinegar is available in liquid form, or in a sachet in powdered form.

- **Sweet rice wine (*mirin*)** This is a sweet rice wine used for cooking only.

- **Toasted sesame seed (*iri goma*)** There are two types of sesame seeds used in Japanese cooking, white and black. You can purchase already toasted sesame seeds in Japanese supermarkets or you can toast them in a dry frying pan.

SMALL
PLATES

JAPANESE EQUIPMENT AND UTENSILS

A Japanese kitchen isn't complete without authentic utensils, including those noted here. However, you could use Le Creuset instead of a nabe pot, or a wok instead of a tempura pan.

- **Chopping board (*manaita*)** For hygiene purposes, glass or plastic is common for domestic use. However, professional Japanese chefs prefer to use wooden boards as wood is gentle on the knife blades and the ingredients do not slip.

- **Cooking chopsticks (*ryori bashi*)** These are longer chopsticks than your average ones, designed specifically for cooking. They are made from strong bamboo and are extremely durable to high heat. These are perfect for use during deep-frying as opposed to using a slotted spoon.

- **Fan (*uchiwa*)** A Japanese fan, often used when making sushi rice (see page 66).

- **Ginger and daikon grater (*oroshiki*)** The very fine-toothed Japanese grater which grates the ginger extremely finely and gives a creamy texture. The larger one is for daikon, a Japanese radish (*mooli*). Both grated ginger and daikon are often used for a garnish.

- **Knives (*houcho*)** An all-purpose knife is most commonly used in the domestic kitchen, whereas 10–15 knives are used in a professional kitchen. It is important to keep the knife sharp with a stone sharpener.

- **Nabe clay pot (*donabe*)** Clay pots are used specifically for nabe dishes, meals cooked at the table by adding vegetables and tofu to a broth. They come in different sizes: a small one serves one person and the larger one serves 10–12 people. The pots can also be used in the oven.

- **Noodle/rice bowl (*donburi*)** As Japanese eat soup, noodles and *donburi* (rice with the toppings) regularly, all households have noodle bowls, which are about 20cm wide and 12cm deep.

- **Omelette pan (*tamagoyaki* pan)** The small rectangular Japanese omelette pan is more common in a domestic setting. The larger square one is for industrial use. Japanese egg rolls cannot be made well without this pan.

- **Pestle and mortar (*suribachi*)** Unlike the Western ones, Japanese mortars have a sharp grating surface inside the bowl. The pestle is made from a hard wood, which works perfectly for grating sesame seeds to a very fine powder.

- **Rice cooker (*suihanki*)** You can cook rice in a heavy-based pan, but if you eat rice at least once or twice a week, it's worth investing in a rice cooker which will make life a hundred times easier. The rice cooker is an essential item in a Japanese kitchen.

- **Sharpening stone (*toishi*)** A rectangular natural stone used to sharpen Japanese knives. It is important to sharpen knives regularly to avoid them being ruined.

- **Sushi barrel (*handai* or *hangiri*)** This piece of kit is the key to making the perfect sushi rice (see also page 66). It is used in combination with a *shamoji* (wooden spatula) and *uchiwa* (fan).

- **Sushi mat (*makisu*)** This is essential equipment for making sushi rolls. It is made up of fine strips of bamboo and is extremely durable.

- **Tempura pan (*tempura nabe*)** A Japanese version of the deep-fryer that is especially practical: there is a rack that sits over the top of the pan on which to rest just-cooked ingredients.

- **Wooden spatula (*shamoji*)** A large, flat spoon used for scooping rice, and mixing sushi rice. It can be made from bamboo, wood or plastic.

- **Wooden sushi mould (*oshi zushi no kata*)** The rectangular wooden mould for making compressed sushi (see page 75). Traditionally, this is soaked in water before using to prevent the sushi rice sticking, otherwise lay clingfilm between the mould and the rice.

GANMODOKI

CRISPY TOFU PATTIES WITH GINGER-SOY DIPPING SAUCE

Ganmodoki (tofu fritters) are one of the most popular tofu appetisers in Japan. Often added to broth and simmered like dumplings, they can also be eaten accompanied only with a dipping sauce as in this recipe. There is something wonderful about the crunch of freshly deep-fried *ganmodoki*.

**SERVES 4 AS A STARTER,
MAKES ABOUT 12 PATTIES**

600g firm tofu
15g dried wakame or a handful
   of rocket or watercress leaves
110ml dashi stock
1 teaspoon soy sauce
1 teaspoon mirin
1 medium carrot, peeled and cut
   into 2.5cm-long matchsticks
1 egg white
2 tablespoons cornflour
1–1.5 litres sunflower or
   vegetable oil, for deep-frying
sea salt and ground white pepper

**FOR THE GINGER-SOY
   DIPPING SAUCE**
120ml soy sauce
60ml rice vinegar
2 tablespoons light brown
   soft sugar
2 tablespoons grated ginger
4 tablespoons grated onion

Combine the ingredients for the dipping sauce at least 30 minutes before serving as this will allow time for the onion to release its sweetness.

Prepare the tofu by wrapping it in a large muslin cloth or clean J-cloth. Holding the tofu over the sink, break it up inside the cloth, squeezing out as much moisture as possible. Tip the crumbled tofu into a large bowl and set aside.

If using wakame, soak the seaweed in a bowl of cold water for 20 minutes or until soft. Gently squeeze out any excess water and set aside.

Heat the dashi stock, soy sauce and mirin in a saucepan over a medium heat. When it simmers, add in the wakame and carrot and cook for 3 minutes, or until the carrots are just cooked and softened. Drain well, and leave in a colander to steam off.

In a bowl, thoroughly mix the egg white, tofu, carrot sticks and wakame or watercress leaves with a pinch of ground white pepper and salt. Check the consistency of the mixture; if it is too wet and soft, add up to a tablespoon of cornflour little by little.

Divide the mixture into 12 portions and form into balls. Use your fingers to slightly flatten the balls into patties. Dust the patties with a little extra cornflour.

Heat the oil for deep-frying in a large pan or wok to 160–170°C. Check the temperature of the oil by dropping a little batter into the oil. At the right temperature, the batter should touch the bottom of the pan then immediately come up naturally to the top without oil spluttering.

Deep-fry the patties for about 2 minutes on each side, or until light golden in colour. Serve immediately with the ginger-soy dipping sauce on the side.

KAKIAGE TEMPURA

Kakiage is an easy tempura that's perfect as a snack or canapé as well as part of a main meal. The crunchy batter on the vegetables with the citrussy soy dipping sauce makes a seductive combo that I just can't stop eating. You can serve the tempura on top of rice or noodle dishes, and it's also nice as a garnish for dishes such as Kitsune Udon (see page 117).

About half an hour before you want to serve this dish, mix all the dipping sauce ingredients together in a small bowl. Leave to sit for the flavours to mingle.

Put the tempura flour in the freezer (keeping it chilled will help with the texture of the batter).

Prepare the vegetables. Slice the mushrooms, yellow pepper and leek into small, thin slices. Make sure to separate the layers of sliced leek. Roughly chop the watercress.

Take the flour out of the freezer and mix with the ice-cold water in a bowl. Add the mushrooms, pepper and leek and mix roughly, taking care not to over-mix. The batter should stick to the vegetables, but should not be too thick. Once all the vegetables are well coated with batter, add the chopped watercress and mix gently.

Heat the oil in a wok or large frying pan to 170°C. Alternatively, check the temperature of the oil by dropping a little batter into the oil. If the batter stays in the bottom of the pan for more than 2 seconds, then the temperature is too low. If the batter floats up immediately and oil spits, then the temperature is too high. At the right temperature, the batter should touch the bottom of the pan then immediately come up naturally to the top without oil spluttering.

Using two tablespoons, scoop the mixture into the hot oil. Do this in batches to avoid overcrowding the pan. Deep-fry for 1–2 minutes, until a light golden colour on both sides. Serve immediately with the dipping sauce alongside.

SERVES 2

100g tempura flour
100g shiitake mushrooms
1 yellow or orange pepper, core and seeds removed
1 leek
handful of watercress
120ml ice-cold water
1–1.5 litres sunflower or vegetable oil, for deep-frying

FOR THE DIPPING SAUCE
6 tablespoons soy sauce
1 tablespoon rice vinegar
2 tablespoons mirin
1 tablespoon lemon juice
2 teaspoons sugar
200g daikon radish, grated

GYOZA DUMPLINGS

Everyone loves gyozas. They make elegant appetisers and are super addictive. Creating delicious vegetarian dumplings took a few goes, but now I know it's more than possible. Filled with nutritious chickpeas, cabbage, sweet corn and mushrooms, these are just as tasty (or perhaps even more so) than their meaty counterparts. This recipe makes a good amount of dumplings so they are perfect for a party. Any extra dumplings can be wrapped and frozen for up to eight weeks. They can be cooked straight from frozen.

MAKES 50–60 DUMPLINGS

50–60 gyoza dumpling
    wrappers
3 tablespoons vegetable or
    sunflower oil
dried chilli flakes to
    serve, optional

FOR THE FILLING
20g dried shiitake mushrooms
80g tinned chickpeas, rinsed
    and drained
80g sweetcorn kernels, roughly
    chopped, or frozen sweetcorn
    kernels, defrosted
80g finely chopped cabbage
4 spring onions, finely chopped
bunch of coriander,
    finely chopped
1 tablespoon grated ginger
1 tablespoon soy sauce
¼ teaspoon ground
    white pepper
1 tablespoon mirin
1 tablespoon sake
1 teaspoon sesame oil
1–2 teaspoons cornflour,
    as needed

FOR THE DIPPING SAUCE
3 tablespoons soy sauce
2 tablespoons rice vinegar
2 tablespoons mirin
2 tablespoons toasted sesame oil

Soak the dried shiitake mushrooms in a bowl of hot water for 1 hour.

Drain the mushrooms, squeeze out any excess water and finely chop. Put the chickpeas in a food processor and pulse to form a relatively smooth texture.

Put the mushrooms and chickpeas, along with the remaining ingredients for the filling and 1 teaspoon of cornflour in a large bowl. Mix well using clean hands. The mixture should be firm enough to form into a ball and not too dry. If the mixture seems too wet, add another teaspoon of cornflour.

Place a dumpling wrapper in the palm of your left hand and dab two-thirds of the edges with water. Place a teaspoonful of the filling in the centre of the wrapper and fold over, making small pinched creases to completely seal the edges together. Repeat with the rest of the filling and wrappers until done.

Heat 2 tablespoons of oil in a large frying pan over a medium-high heat, and then carefully add the dumplings. Pour 120ml of water into the pan and partially cover with the lid, making sure there is a decent gap between the lip of the pan and the lid so that steam can escape. Cook over a medium heat for 5 minutes or until all of the water has evaporated.

Take the lid off and turn up the heat to high, add the remaining 1 tablespoon of oil to the pan, then cook for a further 1 minute or until the base of the dumplings are brown and crisp.

Meanwhile, combine the dipping sauce ingredients in a small bowl.

To serve, use a palette knife to scoop up the dumplings and quickly turn over onto the plate, crispy side up. Serve immediately with the dipping sauce and, if using, the chilli flakes.

TIP

The dumplings keep well frozen. Simply arrange on a tray and put in the freezer for a couple of hours, then transfer to a zip-lock bag. Freeze for up to 3–4 months. Cook the dumplings from frozen following the instructions on page 20. You may need to use slightly a lower heat and cook the dumplings for a bit longer.

ONIGIRI
PURPLE AND GREEN RICE BALLS

Onigiri (rice balls) remain one of the most popular snacks in Japan. Traditionally, they are rice balls with different fillings, but this recipe jumps aboard the new wave of colourful *onigiri*. You can shape the rice mixture into 4 large rice balls, or make 8 smaller ones, which are perfect as canapés. To make them part of a substantial meal, serve with miso soup and tamagoyaki omelette (see page 169).

SERVES 4

Chop the beetroot and turnip stalks into 5–7mm lengths.

In a small bowl, combine the mayonnaise, wasabi and soy sauce.

Heat 1 tablespoon of oil in a frying pan and add the turnip stalks, garlic and spring onions. Gently sauté over a low heat for about 2 minutes. Add half of the mayonnaise-soy mixture and cook for a further 1–2 minutes, until most of the moisture has gone. Transfer to a bowl and set aside.

Quickly wipe the pan with kitchen paper and add the remaining oil. Repeat the above step with the beetroot stalks and the remaining mayonnaise mixture.

Divide the freshly cooked warm rice between 2 bowls. Add the turnip stalk mixture to one bowl and the beetroot mixture to the other. Mix well and season with salt to taste.

Using damp hands, take a quarter of the rice mixture from one bowl and then form a triangular-shaped rice ball, about 3–4cm in thickness. Repeat to make 4 turnip rice balls and 4 beetroot rice balls.

Mix the ao-nori powder with the sesame seeds on a plate. Dip the beetroot rice balls into the ao-nori sesame seed mixture.

Take one of the nori strips and wrap it around the middle of the turnip rice ball. Repeat with all the turnip rice balls.

Serve the purple and green rice balls on a platter.

120g beetroot stalks
120g turnip stalks
4 tablespoons Japanese
 mayonnaise (see page 167)
 or shop-bought mayonnaise
2 teaspoons wasabi paste
4 tablespoons soy sauce
2 tablespoons sunflower or
 vegetable oil
2 garlic cloves, finely chopped
4 spring onions, finely chopped
225g freshly cooked short-grain
 rice (see page 168), still warm
3 tablespoons ao-nori
 (seaweed) powder
2 tablespoons toasted
 sesame seeds
½ nori sheet, cut into 7mm strips
sea salt

QUICK-PICKLED BROCCOLI AND CARROT

This recipe demonstrates the style of preserving fresh ingredients that is well-known throughout Japan and originated in Matsumae in the south-eastern tip of Hokkaido. I love the stickiness and umami introduced by the kombu here.

SERVES 4

20g dried kombu
1 broccoli head (approx. 300–400g), cut into bite-sized pieces
2 carrots, peeled and cut into very fine matchsticks
80g ginger, peeled and finely grated
3 tablespoons soy sauce
1 tablespoon mirin
1 tablespoon plus 1 teaspoon caster sugar
1–2 red chillies, sliced into rounds
80g pickled daikon radish (see page 159), cut into fine matchsticks
1 tablespoon sunflower or vegetable oil
80g walnuts
2 teaspoons shichimi pepper
sea salt

Put 3 tablespoons of cold water in a container and soak the kombu for about 30 minutes, or until soft enough to slice. Remove the kombu, reserving the soaking water, and slice it into very thin pieces against the fibre. Set aside.

Bring a saucepan of salted water to the boil and blanch the broccoli for 2 minutes. Drain and rinse under cold water. Drain again and shake as much water out as possible but do not squeeze the broccoli.

Put the carrots in a bowl and sprinkle with 2 teaspoons of salt. Use clean hands to massage the salt into the carrot for about 3 minutes. The carrot will soften. Rinse well under cold water and leave to drain in a colander. Pat dry with kitchen paper to get rid of any excess moisture.

Add the ginger, soy sauce, mirin, 1 tablespoon of sugar and the chillies to a large bowl. Pour in the reserved kombu soaking water and give it a stir. Add the drained broccoli, carrots, pickled daikon and kombu to the ginger-soy mixture. Leave to marinate for at least 1 hour or up to 2 days.

Heat the oil in a frying pan over a medium heat and fry the walnuts for 5–6 minutes. Add the shichimi pepper, ½ teaspoon of salt and 1 teaspoon of sugar and cook for a further 5–6 minutes, tossing the pan to coat the nuts in the seasonings.

Place the pickled veg mixture in a large bowl to share or in individual bowls. Scatter the toasted walnuts on top.

WINTER SALAD
WITH TAMA-MISO SAUCE

Tama-miso sauce is made using sweet vinegar and miso, thickened with egg yolk. Its rich and silky texture goes very well with any simply cooked chunky chopped vegetables. The sauce also works as a dip for all kinds of crudités. It can be made in advance and stored in the fridge for three to four days.

SERVES 4

4 small beetroot
4 tablespoons olive oil
2 fennel bulbs, leaves intact
½ teaspoon sea salt
240g extra firm tofu, cut into
    large cubes
120g turnip florets, trimmed and
    cut into bite-sized pieces, or
    tenderstem broccoli
4 tablespoons toasted and
    ground sesame seeds

FOR THE TAMA-MISO SAUCE
140g white miso
6 tablespoons rice vinegar
6 tablespoons mirin
1½ tablespoons sugar
2 medium egg yolks
1 teaspoon Dijon mustard or
    ½ teaspoon Japanese mustard

Preheat the oven to 220°C/200°C fan/gas mark 7.

Peel and cut each beetroot into quarters and then rub with a little of the oil. Wrap in a sheet of foil, leaving a tiny gap in the foil for air to escape, and place on a baking sheet. Bake for 45 minutes, or until tender when poked with a fork.

Meanwhile, slice the fennel bulbs along the fibre into chunky segments and then rub with the remaining oil and sprinkle with the salt. Arrange on a roasting tray and cover loosely with foil. Bake for about 20 minutes, or until tender and lightly caramelised. Remove the beetroot and fennel and allow to cool to room temperature.

To make the tama-miso sauce, add all the ingredients except for the mustard to a small saucepan. Set over a very low heat, whisking all the time to prevent the egg yolk from scrambling, and cook for 2–3 minutes until thickened to the consistency of tomato ketchup. Remove from the heat and set aside.

Bring a large pan of water to the boil and add the tofu. Simmer over a medium heat for 2 minutes, then use a slotted spoon to remove. Transfer to kitchen paper to drain. To the same pan of water, add the turnip florets and simmer for 1 minute. Immediately remove the florets from the pan, using a slotted spoon, and plunge into ice-cold water to halt the cooking process. Drain once cooled.

Choose wide and shallow plates or shallow soup bowls for serving. Assemble each plate by placing the beetroot and fennel on first. Coat all surfaces of the tofu squares with ground sesame seeds and then place them on top. Lastly, arrange the turnip florets in the middle and then drizzle the sauce alongside the beetroot and fennel, making sure not to pour it all over the vegetables themselves.

POTATO SALAD

This may sound like a modern Japanese dish, but it is actually a well-established Japanese-Western fusion that has been around in Japan for some time. It's a perfect salad to serve with a deep-fried *katsu* dish to cut through the richness.

SERVES 4

4 medium potatoes, peeled
    and quartered
3 large eggs
2 tablespoons sunflower or
    vegetable oil
100g vegetarian sausage, cut
    into bite-sized pieces
1 cucumber, diced
½ small onion, very thinly sliced
1 carrot, diced
1–2 teaspoons Dijon mustard
6 tablespoons Japanese
    mayonnaise (see page 167)
    or shop-bought mayonnaise
handful of watercress or
    pea shoots
2 tablespoons deep-fried shallots
2 tablespoons teriyaki sauce
    (see page 167), to serve
sea salt and ground white pepper

Bring a large pan of water to the boil and add the potatoes. Simmer over a medium heat for 10 minutes, until just cooked. Drain and return the potatoes to the pan and put back on the heat again for 1 minute for the excess moisture to evaporate. Mash the potatoes roughly and season with salt and white pepper. Set aside.

Place the eggs in a saucepan of water over a medium-high heat. Once it comes to the boil, cook the eggs for 5 minutes. Take off the heat and drain, then plunge into cold water to cool. Peel the eggs and separate the yolks from the whites. Finely chop the whites and crumble the yolks. Set aside.

Heat the oil in a frying pan over a medium heat. Fry the vegetarian sausage for about 2 minutes, until lightly browned. Remove and set aside.

Put the cucumber, onion and carrot in a bowl and sprinkle with a couple pinches of salt. Using clean hands, gently massage the salt into the vegetables for a minute or so until they soften and begin to release water. Rinse under cold water and leave to drain in a colander for 10 minutes. Squeeze out any excess water and pat dry with kitchen paper.

Stir the mustard and mayonnaise through the mashed potatoes and season to taste with salt and pepper.

Add the cucumber, onion, carrot, vegetarian sausage and chopped egg whites to the potato mixture and mix together gently. Garnish the salad with the watercress or pea shoots, crumbled egg yolks and the crispy shallots. Lastly, drizzle with the teriyaki sauce and serve.

SHIRAAE
SPINACH AND TOFU SALAD

Shiraae, a mashed tofu salad, is one of the vegan dishes most eaten by monks. Both the tofu and the miso in the dressing bring a rich and intensely good flavour. It's creamy and delicious.

Konnyaku yam cake is made from konjac yam and has a delightful springy texture. It also comes in noodle form, as used in this recipe.

SERVES 2

Wrap the tofu in muslin cloth and squeeze the excess water out. Break up the tofu in a bowl using a fork, then add the remaining ingredients for the dressing.

Trim off the bottom hard part from the shimeji mushrooms and separate into small bite-sized pieces.

Bring a large pan of salted water to the boil. Add the carrots and shimeji mushrooms and cook for 2 minutes. Use a slotted spoon to transfer the carrots and mushrooms to a bowl of iced water. Add the spinach to the pan and blanch for 20 seconds, then remove with a slotted spoon and drain under cold water until cooled. Drain very well in a colander, then use your hands to squeeze as much excess water out as possible. Roughly chop the spinach and set aside.

Blanch the konnyaku noodles in the same pan for 1 minute and drain in a colander. Set aside.

Drain the carrots and mushrooms and pat dry with kitchen towel. Put into a large bowl and add the spinach, sugar, soy sauce, mirin, konnyaku noodles, shiraae dressing ¼ teaspoon of salt. Toss gently and serve.

80g shimeji mushrooms
1 medium carrot, cut into
    4cm-long matchsticks
150g spinach
100g konnyaku yam noodles, cut
    into 2½cm long matchsticks
1 teaspoon sugar
1 tablespoon soy sauce
1 tablespoon mirin
sea salt

FOR THE SHIRAAE DRESSING
125g silken tofu
1½ teaspoons miso
½ teaspoon tahini
¼ teaspoon sugar
¼ teaspoon salt
1 tablespoon mirin
½ teaspoon rice vinegar
1 teaspoon soy sauce

WARM BUTTERNUT SQUASH AND SUGAR SNAP PEA SALAD

This hearty warm salad is nutrient dense and deeply satisfying. The daikon and ginger dressing gives it a punchy flavour.

SERVES 6

600–700g butternut squash
or ½ kabocha squash
60g enoki mushrooms
300g sugar snap peas
100g tempura flour
175ml ice-cold water
500ml sunflower or vegetable
oil, for deep-frying
2 teaspoons toasted
sesame seeds
handful of pea shoots, to serve
sea salt

**FOR THE DAIKON AND
GINGER DRESSING**
300g daikon radish, finely grated
100g ginger, peeled and
finely grated
125ml sushi vinegar
100ml soy sauce
1 tablespoon toasted and ground
sesame seeds

Mix all the ingredients for the dressing in a bowl. Set aside.

Cut the squash in half and remove the seeds with a spoon. Cut each half into 4 wedges, then slice into 5mm-thick segments (it should look like a crescent shape).

Trim off the bottom part of the enoki mushrooms and separate.

Bring a saucepan of salted water to the boil and blanch the sugar snap peas for 1 minute. Rinse under cold water until cooled, and drain.

Mix the tempura flour and ice-cold water in a bowl to form a slightly runny batter.

Heat the oil in a wok or large frying pan to 180°C using a thermometer. Alternatively, check the temperature of the oil by dropping a little batter into the oil. If the batter stays in the bottom of the pan for more than 2 seconds, then the temperature is too low. If the batter floats up immediately and oil spits, then the temperature is too high. At the right temperature, the batter should touch the bottom of the pan then immediately come up naturally to the top without the oil spluttering.

Dip the squash into the batter and deep-fry for 2–3 minutes, or until the batter becomes a light golden colour. Use a slotted spoon to remove the first batch from the oil, then repeat until all the squash slices are cooked.

Slice the sugar snap peas into 2 or 3 pieces on the diagonal. The peas may pop out but can be randomly placed on the plate together with the sliced pods.

Lay each squash slice on a platter. Pour the dressing over the squash, taking care not to immerse it in the dressing. Decorate the top with the peas, fresh enoki mushrooms, sesame seeds and pea shoots. Serve warm or at room temperature.

BEANSPROUT PANCAKE
WITH MISO-WASABI MAYO

Okonomiyaki is a traditional savoury pancake and literally translates to 'grilled as you like it'. You simply mix in vegetables or whatever you fancy. I have created this lighter version, using only a little flour but plenty of eggs and beansprouts, which go very well together.

SERVES 4

Steam the beansprouts in a steamer for 5 minutes. Alternatively, place the beansprouts in a bowl, cover with clingfilm and microwave for 3 minutes. Leave to cool. When cool enough to handle, drain and squeeze any excess water out gently.

Mix the flour, salt and pepper in a large bowl. Add the eggs, spring onions and drained beansprouts. Stir together well.

In a small bowl, combine the ingredients for the miso-wasabi mayo in a bowl.

Heat 1 tablespoon of oil in a large frying pan over a medium-high heat. Scoop half of the batter into the pan – you're after a thickness of about 1.5cm. Reduce the heat to medium-low and cook for about 5 minutes, or until the bottom is nicely caramelised and has formed a brown crust.

Use a spatula to carefully turn the pancake over and then cook for a further 3–4 minutes or until the other side is nicely dark brown. Keep warm and repeat with the remaining batter.

Remove to a large chopping board and then cut each pancake into 4 or 6 triangular pieces. Arrange on a serving plate and then drizzle over the miso-wasabi mayo. Sprinkle the ao-nori powder over the top and serve.

300g beansprouts
2 tablespoons plain flour
½ teaspoon sea salt
½ teaspoon shichimi pepper, or ground white pepper
2 eggs, lightly beaten
3 spring onions, finely chopped
4 tablespoons sunflower or vegetable oil
2 tablespoons ao-nori (seaweed) powder, to serve

FOR THE MISO-WASABI MAYO
1 tablespoon miso
1 tablespoon mayonnaise
½ teaspoon wasabi paste
1 teaspoon soy sauce
1 teaspoon rice vinegar
1 teaspoon sugar

CHAWANMUSHI
SAVOURY STEAMED EGG CUSTARD

This is a very traditional Japanese dish, which is often served as part of a *kaiseki* meal. Although custard may seem unusual as a savoury offering for Western tastes, this silky savoury custard truly is a splendid way to start a meal.

SERVES 4

5 tablespoons soy sauce
4 tablespoons mirin
80g firm tofu, cut into 1cm cubes
80g broccoli, broken into bite-sized florets
80g shimeji mushrooms
4 large eggs
400ml vegetarian dashi stock (see page 166) or 1 teaspoon kombu dashi powder mixed with 400ml hot water
sea salt

Combine 120ml of water with 3 tablespoons of soy sauce and 2 tablespoons of mirin in a small pan and bring to the boil over a medium heat. Add the tofu cubes and simmer for 3 minutes. Take off the heat and allow to cool.

Place the broccoli in a bowl with a pinch of salt. Pour over enough boiling water to cover and leave to sit for 1 minute. Rinse under cold water and drain. Gently use your hands to squeeze excess water out. Trim the mushrooms by cutting off the thick part of the stems and separate into small bite-sized pieces.

Beat the eggs lightly with a fork in a large bowl. Add the dashi stock and remaining soy sauce and mirin to the eggs, and season with a pinch of salt. Mix well. Pour the mixture through a muslin cloth-lined colander and into a bowl.

Divide the shimeji mushrooms, tofu and broccoli between 4 small heatproof soup bowls or ramekins. Pour the egg mixture into the cups, allowing room for the egg mixture to rise when cooked.

Place in a steamer allowing enough space for steam to circulate between the bowls. Lay a sheet of muslin cloth between the lid and the pan (this will prevent the condensation from dripping into the egg mixture and changing its delicate texture). Bring the water in the steamer to a simmer, reduce the heat, then steam gently over a medium-low heat for 12–13 minutes, or until the custard is just set but not firm. The steaming time will depend on the depth of your bowls.

To check if they are cooked, poke a bamboo skewer into the egg mixture. If a yellow-coloured liquid seeps out, then continue to cook for a couple more minutes. If the liquid is clear, then it is ready.

When they are ready, turn off the heat, leave them to sit for a few minutes, then place them on saucers to serve. Alternatively, the custard can be served chilled in the summer.

KENCHIN-JIRU
MISO AND ROOT VEGETABLE SOUP

Kenchin-jiru is a very traditional soup of tofu and mostly root vegetables. There are two main variants, one with a clear dashi broth and the other with a miso broth. Here is the recipe for a spicy miso version of *kenchin*. Like any hearty soup it will warm you in the winter, but miso also offers health, strength and calm.

SERVES 4

To prepare the tofu, wrap in kitchen paper and press between 2 chopping boards with a weight (such as a tin of beans) on the top. Arrange in the sink on a slight angle, so that excess water can drain away. Leave for 1–2 hours.

Soak the dried mushrooms in a bowl with 200ml of warm water for at least 30 minutes. Drain the mushrooms, reserving the soaking water, discard the stalks and slice the caps thinly.

Meanwhile, soak the burdock in a bowl of cold water for 20 minutes. In a separate bowl, soak the potatoes, daikon and carrot in cold water for 20 minutes to remove the starch. Drain.

Heat the oil in a large pan and fry the burdock, potatoes, daikon and carrot over a medium-high heat for about 3 minutes. Add the mushrooms, along with the reserved mushroom soaking water and stock, turn up the heat to high and bring to the boil. Boil the soup for 2–3 minutes, skimming away any froth on the surface.

In a small bowl, add 2 tablespoons of miso along with about 1 tablespoon of the broth from the pan to loosen. Pour the mixture back into the pan and simmer over a medium heat for a further 20 minutes, until the vegetables are tender and cooked.

Take a ladleful of the broth from the pan and stir this through the remaining miso to loosen it. Pour into the pan and add the chilli bean paste.

Break up the tofu into large bite-sized pieces randomly and then add to the soup. Turn up the heat to high and bring to the boil. Adjust the seasoning by adding more miso or water if it is too salty.

To finish, stir through the chopped spring onions and turn off the heat. Serve immediately.

400g firm tofu
4 dried shiitake mushrooms
100g burdock, peeled
    and cut into small pieces on
    the diagonal
200g potatoes, peeled and cut
    into 2cm cubes
200g daikon radish, peeled
    and cut into small pieces on
    the diagonal
1 medium carrot, peeled
    and cut into small pieces on
    the diagonal
3 tablespoons sesame oil
1.2 litres vegetarian dashi
    stock (see page 166), or
    3 teaspoons kombu dashi
    powder mixed with 1.2 litres
    hot water
100g white miso
1–2 teaspoons chilli bean paste
bunch of spring onions,
    finely chopped

CHINESE CABBAGE AND TOFU CHOWDER

It's hard to believe this rich and creamy dish is vegan. The sweetness and velvety smooth texture of the white miso and almond milk combine so well with the silky tofu. Utterly delicious.

SERVES 4

8 dried shiitake mushrooms
1 Chinese cabbage
400g silken tofu, cut into
    small cubes
60g mangetout, finely sliced
    on the diagonal
300ml vegetarian dashi stock
    (see page 166) or 2 teaspoons
    kombu dashi powder mixed
    with 300ml hot water
60g white miso
2 teaspoons soy sauce
40g ginger, grated
400ml almond milk
200ml sunflower oil, for
    deep-frying
½ leek, thinly sliced
sea salt

Soak the dried shiitake mushrooms in a bowl with 400ml of water for at least 1 hour (or up to about 5 hours). Once the mushrooms are hydrated, drain (reserving the soaking water) and squeeze out any excess water. Slice thinly and set aside.

Slice the cabbage into quarters vertically and then into eighths, making sure all the leaves are attached at the core. Cut the tofu into large bite-sized cubes, taking care not to break them as the tofu is extremely delicate.

In a bowl, sprinkle the mangetout with ½ teaspoon of salt and then pour over enough boiling water to cover. Leave for 1 minute and then drain and rinse under cold water to cool down. Slice thinly and set aside.

Bring the dashi stock and 200ml of the mushroom soaking water to the boil in a large shallow pan. Simmer over a medium heat for about 5 minutes. Skim away any scum that appears on the surface of the stock. Add the miso, soy sauce, ginger, shiitake mushrooms and 1 teaspoon of salt, and bring back to boil.

Add the cabbage pieces, cut-side down and in a single layer, and bring back to the boil. Pour in the almond milk and then turn down the heat to the lowest setting. Cover with a lid or foil, and simmer for about 20 minutes. Make sure the liquid is not boiling otherwise the milk will curdle. Turn the cabbage over and continue to simmer for a further 10 minutes.

Meanwhile, heat the oil in a large pan to 150°C. Carefully add the leek and deep-fry for 30 seconds, until light brown. Remove and drain on kitchen paper.

Carefully take the cabbage pieces out of the pan and then place 2 pieces in each shallow soup bowl, taking care to retain the shape of the cabbage.

Arrange the tofu alongside the cabbage. Pour over the broth and scatter with the sliced mangetout. Sprinkle with the fried leek and serve with spoons and forks or chopsticks.

KABOCHA SQUASH SOUP
WITH TOFU CROUTONS

This soup is a family favourite. It's hard to believe something so rich and creamy uses only Japanese ingredients. The addition of the tofu croutons adds a welcome crunch. You can serve this soup either hot or chilled – both are exquisite.

SERVES 4

To prepare the squash, slice down the middle into halves and then scoop the seeds out with a spoon. Wrap each squash half in clingfilm and cook in the microwave for 2–3 minutes on a high heat (800 watts). Alternatively, steam for 6–8 minutes, or until slightly softened. Peel roughly (there is no need to peel off all of the skin) and then cut into large chunks.

Heat the stock in a large pan over a medium-high heat and bring to the boil. Add the squash to the pan and bring back to the boil. Stir in the mirin, soy sauce and ½ teaspoon of salt and then turn the heat down to medium-low. Simmer for 8–10 minutes, or until the squash is just cooked. To test, insert a skewer into the squash and if it goes in smoothly without any resistance, it is cooked. Take off the heat and allow to cool in the broth.

Meanwhile, make the tofu croutons. Cut the tofu into 1.5cm cubes and pat dry with kitchen paper, dabbing as gently as possible so as not to break up the tofu.

Heat the oil in a small saucepan to 170°C. Mix the cornflour and shichimi pepper on a plate and season with salt. Dust each tofu cube in the seasoned cornflour. Carefully drop into the hot oil and deep-fry for 2–3 minutes, or until light golden all over. Remove with a slotted spoon and drain on kitchen paper.

Transfer the squash and broth to a food processor or blender. Add the almond milk and blitz until you have a smooth and silky consistency. If the mixture seems too stiff, add more milk to loosen.

Reheat the soup gently if serving warm, then divide between individual soup bowls and arrange the tofu croutons in the centre of each bowl. Garnish with the pea shoots and serve.

1 kabocha squash or butternut squash (700–800g)
700ml vegetarian dashi stock (see page 166) or 1½ teaspoons kombu dashi powder mixed with 700ml hot water
60ml mirin
2 tablespoons soy sauce
120ml almond milk or soy milk, plus extra 2–3 tablespoons if needed
handful of pea shoots, to serve
sea salt

FOR THE TOFU CROUTONS
80g extra firm tofu
250ml sunflower or vegetable oil
2–3 tablespoons cornflour
½ teaspoon shichimi pepper

CABBAGE WITH MISO BUTTER

I first had a dish with anchovy butter in Kyoto and it was amazing. The butter infused a simple dish with such deep flavour, and it inspired me to create vegetarian a version, hence the miso butter.

SERVES 2

1 sweetheart cabbage
2 tablespoons vegetable
   or sunflower oil
1 tablespoon pine nuts
2 tablespoons ao-nori
   (seaweed) powder

FOR THE MISO BUTTER
30g red miso
30g unsalted butter, softened
1 tablespoon mirin
2 teaspoons sugar

Cut the cabbage in half vertically. Heat the oil in a large frying pan over a medium heat and then place the cabbage into the pan, cut-side down. Fry for 1 minute and then add 150ml of water to the pan. Turn down the heat to medium-low and then partially cover the pan, allowing steam to escape. Cook for 4–5 minutes, or until the cabbage is just tender.

While the cabbage is cooking, combine the miso, butter, mirin and sugar in a small bowl, making sure there are no lumps. (If you put the mixture in a microwave for 30 seconds, it is easier to mix.)

Check the cabbage – if there is any water in the pan, remove the lid and simmer for a few minutes to allow the water to evaporate completely. Add the miso-butter mixture into the pan and cook, covered, for 2–3 minutes. Remove the lid and allow to cook over a medium-low heat for 2 minutes or until the miso starts to caramelise – check halfway through the cooking time and add a little water to stop the ingredients from burning. When the cabbage is nicely caramelised and sticky, remove from the heat.

Heat a small pan and toast the pine nuts over a low heat for 3–4 minutes.

Place the cabbage halves, cut-side up, on individual plates. Scatter the pine nuts over the cabbage, and sprinkle the ao-nori powder over the top.

GRILLED AUBERGINE
WITH YAKUMI SAUCE

I love, love, love aubergine. It soaks up flavour very well and is simply outstanding grilled. You don't need any other vegetables for this dish. The yakumi sauce and aubergine is a perfect marriage. Just sublime.

SERVES 4

Cut the aubergines in half vertically with the stalk still intact. Preheat the grill to high. Brush the flesh side of the aubergines with the oil and place cut-sides down. Grill for about 15 minutes or until the flesh becomes soft and the skin burnt. Remove and leave to cool.

Combine the ingredients for the sauce in a bowl and leave to sit for at least 30 minutes.

Add the salt to a bowl of water, and soak the shallot slices in it. Grind the toasted sesame seeds using a pestle and mortar.

Once the aubergines are cool enough to handle, peel away the skin. Slice the aubergines in half lengthways, then into large bite-sized chunks or thick slices.

Place the aubergines on a large sharing plate or individual plates and then pour the yakumi sauce over the top. Drain the shallots, pat dry with kitchen paper and sprinkle over the top. Finish with a final scattering of ground sesame seeds and serve at room temperature.

2 large aubergines
2 tablespoons sunflower or
  vegetable oil
½ teaspoon sea salt
2 banana shallots, very
  thinly sliced
2 tablespoons toasted
  sesame seeds

FOR THE YAKUMI SAUCE
4 tablespoons soy sauce
4 tablespoons rice vinegar
1 teaspoon sugar
4 spring onions, finely chopped
2 teaspoons finely chopped or
  grated ginger
1 large red chilli, deseeded and
  finely chopped
1 tablespoon sesame oil

AUBERGINE AND TOFU
WITH MUSTARD MISO

Mustard miso, or *karashi miso* in Japanese, is one of the traditional sauces paired with a variety of dishes in Japan. In this recipe it combines with aubergine and tofu to make a wonderfully full-flavoured dish.

SERVES 2

150g firm tofu, cut into 2cm cubes
100g mangetout
6 tablespoons sunflower or
    vegetable oil
8 spring onions, white and
    green parts separated and
    finely chopped
1 aubergine, cut into 2cm cubes
3 tablespoons toasted and
    ground sesame seeds, to serve
sea salt and ground white pepper

FOR THE MUSTARD MISO
80g white miso
2 tablespoons rice vinegar
2 teaspoons soy sauce
3 teaspoons sugar
1½ teaspoons Dijon mustard

Put the tofu cubes in a clean tea towel or on a few layers of kitchen paper and pat dry.

Bring a pan of salted water to the boil and add the mangetout. Blanch for about 30 seconds, then drain and rinse under cold water. Set aside.

Mix all the mustard miso ingredients in a small bowl and set aside.

Heat 4 tablespoons of the oil in a large wok or frying pan over a medium heat and then add the white part of the spring onions, and the aubergine. Stir-fry for 3–4 minutes.

Add the remaining 2 tablespoons of oil, the tofu and green parts of the spring onions and stir-fry for 2 minutes.

Add in the mustard miso mixture and a pinch of salt and pepper. Stir-fry for another 2 minutes, turn off the heat and stir in the mangetout. Divide between individual bowls and then sprinkle with ground sesame seeds.

MISO

High in protein and rich in vitamins, miso is a Japanese seasoning traditionally made from fermented soybeans, salt and *koji* (a mould starter) and sometimes with rice, barley or seaweed too. In both modern and traditional Japanese cooking, this rich, savoury paste seasons a dish with its incredible umami flavour. Because of this, miso plays a particularly important role in vegetarian cooking.

The taste, aroma, texture and appearance of miso vary by region and season. It is typically thought of as salty, but its flavour depends on factors such as the ingredients and fermentation process. Because of the myriad varieties, miso has been described as salty, sweet, earthy, fruity and savoury.

Although white (*shiro*) and red (*aka*) miso are available throughout the country, they are differentially preferred across the regions of Japan: red miso is most popular in the eastern regions, while in the west there is a preference for white miso. In this book, if the recipes doesn't specify the kind of miso then use any kind you like.

White miso is the most widely produced and consists of mainly rice, barley and a small quantity of soybeans. Compared to red miso, white miso has a very short fermentation time and tastes sweet. The umami profile is soft and light.

Red miso is aged, sometimes for more than a year, and during this time the colour changes gradually from white to red or black, thus the name. It is often a much stronger-tasting miso.

Awase (or mixed) miso comes in many types, because it is a mixture or compound of other varieties of miso.

USEAGE

- Miso typically comes as a paste in a sealed container requiring refrigeration after opening.

- In Japanese cuisine, miso is of course used in soup but it is also commonly used to cure ingredients as a marinade, flavouring food or making sauces. This slow process helps the umami flavour come through more intensely. For example, see the Miso-cured Tofu on page 148, my absolute favourite recipe in this book.

- In cooked dishes such as soups and noodles, the precious umami flavour of miso can be lost if it is overcooked. I believe it's always best to add the miso just before you remove the pot from the heat, giving it a chance to melt or heat through briefly.

- Soy miso is often used to make a pickle called *misozuke*, which is typically made using cucumber, daikon, cabbage or aubergine. *Misozuke* is sweeter than your standard Japanese salted pickle.

ROASTED CAULIFLOWER STEAK
WITH MISO SWEETCORN BUTTER

Miso and sweetcorn is a match made in heaven for modern Japanese cuisine. And nothing soaks up those intense flavours like cauliflower, while taking on their appetising golden colour. The samphire flash-fried with toasted sesame seeds completes the dish.

SERVES 4

2 cauliflower heads
4 tablespoons sunflower
  or vegetable oil
½ teaspoon sea salt
½ teaspoon shichimi pepper
180g samphire
15g butter
2 tablespoons toasted
  sesame seeds
100g sweetcorn, drained

FOR THE MISO-SWEETCORN BUTTER
100g miso
300g tinned sweetcorn, drained
6 tablespoons mirin
30g butter, softened

Trim off the cauliflower leaves and most of the lower part of the stems, leaving enough of each stem to keep the florets intact. Place the whole cauliflowers, stem-side down, on a chopping board and slice into 4 thick slices, making sure each slice is the same thickness.

Place all the ingredients for the miso-sweetcorn butter in a food processor and blitz until you have a smooth texture. Set aside.

Preheat the oven to 220°C/200°C fan/gas mark 7.

Heat 3 tablespoons of the oil in a large frying pan over a medium heat. Place the cauliflower steaks in the pan, then season with the salt and shichimi pepper. Cook for 2 minutes and then turn over and cook the other side for 1 minute.

Transfer the cauliflower steaks to a roasting tray and spread each steak with a thick layer of the miso-sweetcorn butter, leaving about 1cm around the edge of each steak. Bake for about 10 minutes, checking halfway through that it's not burning. If so, turn down the oven temperature or cover the cauliflower with foil.

Meanwhile, place the samphire in a bowl and then pour boiling water over the top. Allow to soak for 1 minute. Drain and then transfer the samphire to a bowl of ice-cold water. Drain again and leave in a colander.

Check the cauliflower – the miso-sweetcorn mixture should be bubbling and slightly darkened in colour. Remove from the oven.

Heat a frying pan with the 15g of butter and remaining 1 tablespoon of oil and add the samphire and sesame seeds. Toss and cook, over a high heat, for 30 seconds. Remove from the heat.

Arrange the cauliflower steaks on serving plates and top with the samphire and sweetcorn.

MISO TOFU AND AUBERGINE

This miso-enriched sauce is the perfect coating for tofu and aubergine. Rice or noodles make a fine accompaniment if you want to serve it as a main meal.

SERVES 4

2 large aubergines
6 tablespoons sunflower
    or vegetable oil
400g firm tofu
4 spring onions, finely chopped,
    green and white parts
    separated
4 shiitake mushrooms,
    stalks removed and caps
    finely chopped
1 red chilli, finely chopped
½ teaspoon sea salt
½ teaspoon ground
    white pepper
2 tablespoons toasted sesame
    seeds, to serve

FOR THE MABO SAUCE
40g red miso
2 tablespoons sake
2 tablespoons mirin
2 tablespoons soy sauce
2 teaspoons sugar
1 teaspoon cornflour
1 tablespoon sesame oil

Cut each aubergine in half vertically, keeping the stalks intact.

Heat 2 tablespoons of the oil in a large frying pan over a medium heat and then place the aubergines, cut-side down, into the pan. Cover with foil or a tight-fitting lid and reduce the heat to medium-low. Cook for 5–6 minutes, taking care not to burn the aubergines.

Turn the aubergine halves over and add another 2 tablespoons of oil. Cook for a further 3–4 minutes, uncovered, or until the aubergines are tender and cooked through. Remove to a plate with the cut sides facing up, and keep warm.

Place the tofu in a muslin cloth or clean J-cloth and squeeze out excess water, crumbling it as you do so.

Mix all the sauce ingredients with 80ml of water in a small bowl and set aside.

Heat the remaining 2 tablespoons of oil in a wok or large frying pan. Add the spring onions (reserving a small amount of the greens to garnish), mushrooms, chilli and crumbled tofu. Season with the salt and pepper, and stir-fry for 3–4 minutes.

Add the sauce to the wok and turn the heat up to high. Stir-fry for 2–3 minutes, until most of the moisture has evaporated.

Scoop out the tofu mixture and place on top of the aubergines. Sprinkle over the reserved green parts of the spring onions and finally top with the sesame seeds.

RED MISO AND HIJIKI ARANCINI

Following the success of the miso arancini with mushrooms from my last book, *Cook Japan*, I'm introducing another arancini recipe, and one with bolder flavours. The deep saltiness of red miso and sweetness of the hijiki seaweed are reminiscent of miso soup. It's a great example of Japan meets Italy: Japanese ingredients cooked the Italian way.

MAKES 24

Wash the rice, and add to a saucepan with 500ml of water and soak for at least 30 minutes or up to 2 hours.

Combine the miso with the mirin in a small bowl and mix to loosen. Add the dashi powder and mix well.

Add the spring onions, hijiki seaweed and miso mixture to the pan with the rice and water. Cook the rice as per the instructions on page 168 (alternatively, use a rice cooker) for 15 minutes.

When the rice is cooked, turn off the heat and leave it to sit with the lid on for 10–15 minutes.

Then stir the rice and transfer to a large shallow dish. Spread the rice mixture to form an even layer, then leave to cool to room temperature. Beat 1 egg, and add to the rice. Mix well.

Using damp hands, form ping-pong-sized balls and press your thumb into each ball to make an indentation. Push a cube of mozzarella into each indentation then mould the rice mixture around to seal. Make sure the mozzarella is completely covered and encased in the rice.

Mix the flour, salt, white pepper, breadcrumbs and ao-nori powder on a plate. Whisk the remaining 2 eggs in a bowl.

Heat the oil in a wok or a large frying pan to 180°C. Dip each rice ball into the eggs first, then into the breadcrumb mixture to coat. Carefully drop the balls, in batches, into the hot oil. Deep-fry for about 2 minutes, or until the balls are golden. Remove with a slotted spoon and drain on kitchen paper for 2 minutes. Serve the arancini with the mayonnaise on the side, and the watercress, if using.

450g short-grain rice
40g red miso
2 teaspoons mirin
1 teaspoon kombu dashi powder
6 spring onions, finely chopped
20g dried hijiki seaweed
3 eggs
100g mozzarella, cut into small cubes
4 tablespoons plain flour
½ teaspoon sea salt
¼ teaspoon ground white pepper
300g panko breadcrumbs
2–3 tablespoons ao-nori (seaweed) powder
1 litre sunflower or vegetable oil, for deep-frying
4 tablespoons wasabi mayonnaise (see page 141) or yuzu mayonnaise (see page 144)
handful of watercress or pea shoots

FRIED TOFU YAKITORI

Yakitori is of course skewered chicken grilled over charcoal, and some would prefer the word not to be used outside of this context. This dish, though, matches the original in shape, colour and flavour. It deserves to steal the name. Deep-fried tofu cubes can be bought as a block and makes this quick dish easy work – and so juicy!

SERVES 4

500ml vegetarian dashi stock
   (see page 166), or 1 teaspoon
   kombu dashi powder mixed
   with 500ml hot water
80ml soy sauce
1 tablespoon sugar
4 tablespoons mirin
2 tablespoons sake
300g deep-fried tofu cubes
2 tablespoons vegetable or
   sunflower oil
1 green pepper, stalk and core
   removed, cut into large pieces
1 red pepper, stalk and core
   removed, cut into large pieces
1 yellow pepper, stalk and core
   removed, cut into large pieces
1 tablespoon black and/or white
   sesame seeds
sea salt

TO SERVE
sansho pepper
shichimi pepper

YOU WILL NEED
4 wooden skewers, soaked
   in hot water for 30 minutes
   before using

Heat the dashi stock, soy sauce, sugar, mirin, sake and a pinch of salt in a large pan and bring to the boil.

Meanwhile, pour boiling water over the deep-fried tofu and leave to sit for 5 minutes. This step will remove excess grease from the tofu. Drain and gently squeeze out any excess water.

Add the tofu cubes to the stock and immediately turn the heat down. Cook for 15–20 minutes, stirring occasionally, until the tofu soaks up some of the stock. Turn off the heat and leave the tofu in the pan to cool – it will continue to drink up the stock during this time.

Heat 1 tablespoon of the oil in a frying pan and stir-fry the peppers for 4–5 minutes. Remove from the pan and set aside to cool.

Thread a tofu cube onto the skewer followed by a pepper piece, then alternate until the skewer is full, leaving 5cm at one end and finishing with a piece of tofu.

Heat a large frying pan with the remaining oil and arrange the skewers in the pan. Allow to heat through over a medium heat for 2 minutes on each side until slightly caramelised. Alternatively, place under a grill.

Plate up and sprinkle over the sesame seeds. Serve immediately with sansho pepper and/or shichimi pepper on the side.

DENGAKU MISO TOFU

This is one of the most famous and authentic Japanese tofu dishes. *Dengaku* is a traditional sweet miso mixture that is very versatile and has a complex flavour profile. It comes in various colours and can be bought ready-made in Japan but it's very easy to make as in this recipe.

SERVES 4

600g firm tofu

FOR THE WHITE AND GREEN DENGAKU MISO
100g white miso
1 tablespoon mirin
1 tablespoon sugar
1 egg yolk
8 shiso leaves or 20g coriander leaves, plus extra to garnish

FOR THE RED DENGAKU MISO
50g red miso
3 tablespoons mirin
1 tablespoon sugar

To prepare the tofu, wrap in kitchen paper and press between 2 chopping boards with a weight (such as a tin of beans) on the top. Arrange in the sink on a slight angle, so that excess water can drain away. Leave for 1–2 hours.

To make the white dengaku miso, combine the white miso, mirin, sugar and 4 tablespoons of water in a small saucepan and set over a low heat. Simmer for about 5 minutes, mixing all the time until thickened and sticky. Turn off the heat and let cool briefly. Put the egg yolk in a bowl, then gradually whisk in the miso mixture, making sure there are no lumps.

To make the green dengaku miso, tear the shiso leaves or coriander leaves into small pieces and grind in a mortar and pestle until you have a smooth and thick paste. Add half of the white dengaku miso and mix well.

To make the red dengaku miso, combine the red miso, mirin, sugar and 5 tablespoons of water in a saucepan and place over a low heat. Simmer for 5–6 minutes, or until shiny and thick (a mayonnaise-like consistency). Take off the heat and allow to cool to room temperature, at which point it will thicken further.

Preheat the grill to medium-high. Cut the tofu into 12 squares and grill for about 5 minutes, then turn over and grill for a further 3 minutes.

Remove the tofu squares from the grill and spread 4 tofu cubes with the white dengaku miso. Take another 4 tofu squares and spread them with the green dengaku miso; repeat with the red dengaku and the remaining squares. Place the tofu squares back under the grill for 2–3 minutes, or until the miso starts bubbling and caramelising slightly.

Serve garnished with extra shiso leaves.

AGEDASHI TOFU

I made a slight tweak to the traditional agedashi tofu (deep-fried tofu in dashi broth) recipe and transformed it into this recipe packed with colour and nutrition. It's a very pretty starter for a dinner party. I love the texture and variety of flavours in this dish and I hope you will too.

SERVES 4

2 x 300g firm tofu blocks
880ml vegetarian dashi stock
    (see page 166) or 1 teaspoon
    kombu dashi powder mixed
    with 880ml hot water
3 tablespoons soy sauce
2 tablespoons sake
3 tablespoons mirin
1 litre sunflower or vegetable oil,
    for deep-frying
80g cornflour
12 small green peppers
    (padrón peppers)
12 baby corn, halved vertically
2 tablespoons grated
    daikon radish
2 tablespoons grated carrot
2 tablespoons grated ginger
sea salt

To prepare the tofu, wrap in kitchen paper and press between 2 chopping boards with a weight (such as a tin of beans) on the top. Arrange in the sink on a slight angle, so that excess water can drain away. Leave for 1–2 hours.

In a saucepan, combine the dashi stock, soy sauce, sake, mirin and a pinch of salt, and bring to the boil over a medium-high heat. Reduce the heat to low and simmer for 5–6 minutes. Turn off the heat.

Meanwhile, remove the board and weights from the tofu blocks and cut each block of tofu into 6 chunks.

Heat the oil in a wide and deep pan or large wok until it reaches 160°C.

Mix the cornflour with a pinch of salt and set aside a couple of tablespoons for later. Pat the tofu pieces dry using kitchen paper and dust with the cornflour. Add the tofu pieces to the oil and deep-fry for 2–3 minutes, turning halfway through the cooking time, until light golden in colour. Remove with a slotted spoon and drain on kitchen paper.

Deep-fry the green peppers and baby corn for 1–2 minutes, until just cooked and bright in colour. Remove and drain on kitchen paper.

Heat the broth and bring back to the boil. Take the reserved cornflour and combine with 4 tablespoons of water in a small bowl. Pour this mixture into the broth and simmer for 1 minute, stirring all the time.

Place 3 tofu pieces in individual shallow bowls and arrange the green peppers and baby corn alongside. Slowly pour the broth into the bowl, taking care not to pour it over the tofu or veg. Place the grated daikon, carrot and ginger atop of the tofu to finish.

SUSHI RICE

Traditionally, the wooden barrel known as a *hangiri* or *handai* is used for transferring cooked rice – and tossing it with the seasonings – when making sushi. A large, flat-bottomed bowl and a wooden spatula will do the trick too.

MAKES 1.2–1.4KG SUSHI RICE – ENOUGH TO SERVE 4–6

640g short-grain rice

SEASONING
220ml rice vinegar
120g caster sugar
1 teaspoon sea salt
1 teaspoon kombu dashi powder or liquid concentrated vegetarian dashi stock

USEFUL EQUIPMENT
handai or *hangiri*, or a large wooden barrel
flat wooden spatula
large fan

Put all the seasoning ingredients into a saucepan and heat gently, stirring to dissolve the sugar and salt. Simmer gently over a low heat for about 5 minutes, or until slightly thickened.

Measure out the rice in the saucepan you will use to cook it with. Rinse the rice in cold water and drain. Repeat this 3 or 4 times until the water becomes almost clear. Add 1.1 litres of cold water and leave to soak for at least 30 minutes or up to 5 hours.

Cover the pan tightly and bring to the boil over a medium-high heat. Reduce the heat and simmer, covered, for 13–16 minutes or until the water is absorbed. Don't be tempted to lift off the lid otherwise the steam will escape. Remove from the heat, and then allow the rice to stand for 15 minutes with the lid on.

Tip the cooked rice into a large, flat-bottomed bowl (preferably wooden) and spread out in the bowl while the rice is steaming hot. Gradually pour in the sushi seasoning and, using a large wooden flat spatula, on a slight angle, cut through the lumps of rice and fold the rice over itself. Avoid using a stirring motion as this will flatten the grains and makes the sushi rice lumpy. Continue folding the rice gently and use your other hand to fan the rice until cooled to room temperature. Fanning is a very important step because cooling the rice quickly will make it shiny and sticky. Cover with a damp cloth until needed. You can make this up to 3 hours in advance.

NIGIRI
HAND-MOULDED SUSHI

Nigiri, or hand-moulded, sushi, this is what I call the king of sushi. It is the most traditional and most well known variety. If you say 'sushi' in Japan you mean *nigiri*. You can choose to make as many *nigiri* as you like and mix and match the below ingredients.

MAKES 16 PIECES

Have a small bowl of cold water at the ready.

For each piece of sushi, dip your leading hand into the bowl of cold water, scoop up about 1 tablespoon of sushi rice (aim for each rice ball to weigh 15–20g), then gently but firmly mould the rice into a ball, making it slightly oval in shape. Do not squash the rice but make sure the grains stick together firmly. The size of the rice ball must be smaller than the topping.

Take your topping with the other hand and then place on top of the rice ball. Then, press together lightly – the topping should be elegantly draped over the rice, not sitting on top of the rice. Wrap a strip of nori around the rice and topping and press to secure underneath.

Serve with the soy sauce, pickled ginger and wasabi.

320g sushi rice (see page 66)

CHOICE OF TOPPINGS
pickled daikon radish (see page 159), cut into 2cm-wide strips
pickled fennel and courgette (see page 162)
shiitake mushrooms, fried in a dash of oil for 5 minutes over a low heat
smoked tofu, cut into 2cm-wide strips
deep-fried tofu, cut into 2cm-wide strips
avocado, destoned and flesh cut into 2cm-wide strips
roasted peppers, cut into 2cm-wide strips
tamagoyaki omelette (see page 169)
2 nori sheets, cut into thin ribbons

TO SERVE
soy sauce
pickled ginger
wasabi

INARI SUSHI

Deep-fried tofu stuffed with rice is a classic everyday type of sushi. Tofu sheets are deep-fried and sweetened, and when paired with the sushi rice it makes for a juicy and delicious morsel. Inari sushi was my morning snack during my high school years.

MAKES 20 PIECES

4 dried shiitake mushrooms
1 carrot, peeled and cut into matchsticks
10 deep-fried tofu sheets (available from Japanese supermarkets)
500ml vegetarian dashi stock (see page 166), or 2 teaspoons kombu dashi powder mixed with 500ml hot water
120ml soy sauce
2 tablespoons mirin
2 tablespoons sake
2 tablespoons sugar
100g tinned bamboo shoots, drained and cut into matchsticks
80g mangetout
650g sushi rice (see page 66)
1 tablespoon toasted sesame seeds
pickled ginger, to serve
sea salt

Soak the shiitake mushrooms in 250ml of hot water for at least 1 hour with a pinch of sugar. Remove the mushrooms and reserve the soaking liquid.

Bring a small saucepan of water to the boil and cook the carrots for 3 minutes. Drain.

Pour boiling water over the deep-fried tofu sheets to remove excess grease. Cut each in half to make even square pieces.

Bring the dashi stock to the boil in a large saucepan and then add the soy sauce, mirin, sake and sugar. Add the shiitake mushrooms and their soaking liquid, bamboo shoots, cooked carrot and deep-fried tofu squares. Cut a round of parchment paper the same circumference as the pan and place on top of the ingredients in the pan – it should just touch the surface of the liquid. Cover with the lid and simmer over a low heat for about 15 minutes, making sure to check there is enough liquid. Add a little water if it becomes dry. Turn off the heat and let cool in the pan.

Meanwhile, bring a small saucepan of salted water to the boil cook the mangetout for 2 minutes. Drain and rinse under running cold water until the mangetout have cooled. Drain and set aside.

Drain the stock, reserving the vegetables and tofu. Squeeze the liquid out of the shiitake mushrooms, then very thinly slice them. Finely chop the carrots and bamboo shoots. Add the mushrooms, carrot and bamboo to the sushi rice and mix gently, breaking up any lumps. Add the toasted sesame seeds and mix.

Gently squeeze the deep-fried tofu to release any excess liquid, but they should still be moist. Carefully prise open the cut side of each tofu square, being careful not to tear the sheet. You should have tofu pockets. Turn 10 of the pockets inside out – leaving you with 2 different outside surface textures. Stuff the rice mixture into 10 of the pockets and close. Place the sushi on a board, closed-side down.

Stuff the remaining rice mixture into the rest of the tofu pockets and leave the tops open to expose the rice. Tuck the edges in to reveal the rice mixture. Serve alongside the mangetout and pickled ginger.

OSHI ZUSHI
COMPRESSED SUSHI

Oshi zushi is compressed sushi – the word *oshi* means press or push. This is the oldest sushi, and originally it was a method for preserving fish. Traditionally, pickled fish is used but I'm introducing a vegetarian version here that I think works very well in lunchboxes and as a canapé.

MAKES ABOUT 64 PIECES

1 large red pepper
1 large yellow pepper
600g sushi rice (see page 66)
120g cream cheese
1 tablespoon finely chopped
    green parts of spring onions,
    or chives

TO SERVE
soy sauce
pickled ginger
wasabi

To roast the peppers, preheat the oven to 200°C/180°C fan/gas mark 6. Place the whole peppers on an oven tray and bake for about 30 minutes, then give them a turn and bake for a further 10 minutes. Remove and leave to cool. Peel and cut them into half. Take the cores and seeds out and then cut each half into 3 strips.

Line the inside of a 20 x 10cm loaf tin with clingfilm leaving plenty of overhang.

Take about 225g sushi rice and press into the lined container, spreading it as evenly as possible. In a bowl, combine the cream cheese with the chopped spring onions and spread the mixture over the rice.

Place the remaining sushi rice on top of the cream cheese mixture and pat over the top evenly, then press down on it to compress. Lay strips of red and yellow roasted peppers on top of the rice, alternating the colours to form a pattern as you go.

Cover the surface with the clingfilm and use the palms of your hands to press down firmly. Place a few tins (such as tinned beans or tomatoes) on top and leave to sit in a cool place for at least 2 hours to compress – this step also allows the rice to absorb the flavours of the topping.

When ready to serve, holding the clingfilm, lift the whole block of sushi out from the tin. Remove the clingfilm carefully, then slice the sushi into 2.5cm cubes or large bite-sized pieces. Serve with the condiments of choice.

URAMAKI ZUSHI
INSIDE-OUT SUSHI

Also known as 'California roll', this form of sushi was invented in the early 70s. One of the classic fillings is crab, avocado and mayonnaise but the inside-out sushi is more a style of rolling and you can use any fillings you like.

MAKES ABOUT 64 PIECES

3 dried shiitake mushrooms
2 tablespoons soy sauce
2 tablespoons mirin
3 teaspoons miso
1 teaspoon sugar
1 avocado
4 nori sheets, each cut in half
650g sushi rice (see page 66)
2 tablespoons toasted black and
   white sesame seeds
80g smoked tofu, cut into
   1cm batons
80g pickled daikon radish,
   cut into 1cm batons
   (see page 159)
3 tablespoons wasabi
   mayonnaise (see page 141)
2 vegetarian sausages, cut into
   1cm batons
½ cucumber, cut into 1cm batons

First, prepare the filling for the sushi. Soak the mushrooms in a bowl with 250ml of hot water. Leave for 15 minutes.

Drain the mushrooms (reserving about 120ml of the soaking liquid) and squeeze out any excess water. Trim away the stems and slice the caps into about 1cm-thick pieces.

Place the mushrooms in a small saucepan with the soaking water, soy sauce and mirin. Heat gently and cook for 5–6 minutes. Take off the heat and allow the mushrooms to cool in the pan. Once the mushrooms are cool enough to handle, remove and squeeze out any excess moisture.

In a small bowl, combine the miso with the sugar. Cut the avocado in half first, remove the stone and slice the flesh into segments about 1cm thick.

To assemble the sushi, place one nori half lengthways on a bamboo sushi mat. Have a small bowl of cold water at the ready. Dip your hands in the cold water, shake off the excess, then scoop up a handful of the sushi rice. Spread the rice over the nori sheet, covering it evenly and leave a 5cm border on the side furthest from you. Press the rice gently to smooth out the surface but do not use too much force. The thickness of the rice should be around 7mm.

Sprinkle over some of the sesame seeds and cover with a layer of clingfilm. Place another bamboo sushi mat over the rice, then turn over and take off the bamboo mat previously on the underside.

You will be making rolls with 2 sets of fillings. For the first one, spread a little of the sweetened miso over the nori sheet in the centre from left to right. Arrange the shiitake mushrooms, smoked tofu and pickled daikon on top. For the second filling, spread a little wasabi mayonnaise over the nori sheet, then arrange the avocado, sausage and cucumber pieces on top.

To roll the sushi rolls up, using both hands, pick up the sides of the sushi mat and clingfilm closest to you with your index fingers and thumbs. Carefully roll up the nori sheet (using the mat and clingfilm as a guide), enclosing the filling (but not the clingfilm) inside the nori sheet as you roll, rolling away from you and toward the far side. Try your best to roll as tightly as possible. Unroll the mat only but keep the sushi roll in the clingfilm. Carefully peel away the clingfilm, keeping the sushi roll in place, then use a sharp knife to cut the roll into 8 pieces. Repeat with the remaining nori, rice and fillings.

To finish, add a small dollop of the sweetened miso on each piece of sushi.

TEMPURA MAKI

This is a deep-fried battered sushi roll, believe or not. It's so tasty. The secret is to make sure the batter is very thin as this ensures a light and oh-so-crispy coating for the roll.

Combine the miso and mirin in a bowl until smooth. Add the blanched watercress and stir to combine, then set aside.

Have a bowl of cold water at the ready. Place a bamboo sushi mat on the bench top. Place one nori sheet on the mat, rough side up. Dip your hands in the cold water, shake off any excess water, and then scoop up a large handful of sushi rice.

Spread the rice over the nori sheet to cover it evenly, leaving about a 5cm border on the side furthest from you. Use your hands to press down firmly to smooth the surface of the rice.

You will be making 2 sets of fillings. For the first kind, add the some of the smoked tofu and watercress-miso mixture. For the second, add some avocado, roasted pepper and wasabi mayonnaise. Arrange the fillings horizontally in a row across the centre of the rice. Cut off the excess if the strips of filling ingredients are too long.

Hold the bamboo sushi mat using both hands and carefully roll up, tucking the fillings in so that they remain in the middle. Roll away from the side closest to you, using both hands to firmly squeeze the roll. Repeat the process to make 8 rolls in total, 4 of each kind of filling.

Heat enough oil to come 2–3cm up the sides of a deep, wide frying pan to 170°C. Cut each of your rolls in half.

In a bowl, combine the tempura flour and ice-cold water to make a batter. Dip the sushi roll into the batter and coat. Then immediately and carefully slide the roll into the hot oil. Repeat with the remaining sushi rolls, taking care not to overcrowd the pan. Deep-fry for 2 minutes, until lightly golden. Remove with a slotted spoon and drain on kitchen paper.

Take a sharp knife and wipe it with a damp cloth, then use to slice the sushi rolls into bite-sized pieces. Serve the delectable morsels with ponzu dipping sauce on the side.

MAKES ABOUT 64 PIECES

8 nori sheets
450g sushi rice (see page 66)
1 litre vegetable or sunflower oil, for deep-frying
100g tempura flour
250ml ice-cold water
80ml ponzu dipping sauce (see page 167), to serve

FOR THE SMOKED TOFU AND WATERCRESS FILLING

1 tablespoon red miso
1 teaspoon mirin
40g watercress, blanched in boiling water for 20 seconds, drained and rinsed under cold water
40g smoked tofu, cut into thin strips

FOR THE AVOCADO AND ROAST PEPPER FILLING

1 small avocado, stone removed and flesh cut into thin strips
1 roasted red pepper, peeled and cut into thin strips
2 tablespoons wasabi mayonnaise (see page 141)

TEZUNA ZUSHI
ROPED SUSHI

Known as *tezuna zushi* in Japan, this is a completely new style of sushi. It's like a sushi roll without the nori sheet. Making the pattern in the photograph is a little tricky and might take some patience but it's so pretty once you master it.

MAKES ABOUT 64 PIECES

4 dried shiitake mushrooms
1 carrot, peeled, cut into
    12cm lengths and very finely
    sliced into ribbons
3 baby courgettes, or
    1 courgette, very fine
    sliced into ribbons
120ml soy sauce
2 tablespoons mirin
2 tablespoons sugar
1 deep-fried tofu sheet
1 avocado
½ teaspoon rice vinegar or
    lemon juice
handful of coriander
    leaves, chopped
450g sushi rice (see page 66)
1 small red chilli, finely sliced
1 tablespoon toasted
    sesame seeds
sea salt

Soak the shiitake mushrooms in a bowl with 250ml of hot water for 15 minutes. Drain the mushrooms, reserving the soaking liquid, and gently squeeze out any excess moisture from the mushrooms. Set aside.

Bring a pan of salted water to the boil over a medium heat. Place the finely sliced carrot and courgettes into the pan and boil for 1 minute. Remove from the pan, drain and pat dry with kitchen paper.

In a saucepan, heat the soy sauce, mirin and sugar with the reserved shiitake soaking water over a medium-high heat. Once it has come to the boil, add the deep-fried tofu sheet and shiitake mushrooms. Reduce the heat to medium-low, cover the pan with a lid and simmer for 15–20 minutes or until the liquid has reduced down by about 80 per cent. Take the pan off the heat and allow the ingredients to cool.

In a bowl, peel and roughly mash the avocado with the rice vinegar or lemon juice (this prevents the avocado from discolouring) and mix in the chopped coriander.

Once the mushrooms and tofu are cool, squeeze to remove excess moisture. Cut the tofu in half and then prise open the sheets (if it's too difficult to separate the layers, then just leave it as it is) and cut into 12cm x 2cm ribbons, around the same size as the courgette and carrot.

Trim the stems from the shiitake mushrooms and chop the caps finely. Add the shiitake mushrooms to the avocado mixture and combine well.

Place a bamboo sushi mat on the bench top and line with a sheet of clingfilm, leaving a bit of overhang at the edge closest to you. Place a chopstick (or wooden skewer) on the clingfilm, leaving about a 5cm gap from the edge closest to you (this will help work as a guide to keep the veg straight). Add a couple of pieces each of courgette, carrot and tofu in a kind of backward slash fashion, alternating the ingredients.

Have a small bowl of cold water at the ready. Dip your hands in the water and grab a small handful of sushi rice, flattening it as much as possible in your hands. Place the flattened sushi rice on top of the vegetables. Spread a layer of the avocado and shiitake mixture on top of the rice followed by another thin layer of sushi rice. Press down gently.

Take the chopstick/skewer out and then, holding the bamboo sushi mat and clingfilm together with both hands, carefully roll the whole thing up. Once it is rolled, press and squeeze towards the edges. Remove the bamboo mat, leaving the clingfilm layer on. Repeat with the remaining ingredients to make 8 rolls.

Wipe a sharp knife with a damp cloth and use to slice the rolls into 8 pieces. Peel off the clingfilm and serve, scattered with the chilli and sesame seeds.

CHIRASHIZUSHI
SCATTERED SUSHI

Chirashizushi is the most popular home-style sushi in Japan. Kansai (West Japan) and Kanto (East Japan) styles are different, with the Kanto style focused on raw fish and Kansai more open to diversity. I have created a third variety with vibrant vegetables, pickled lotus root, marinated mushrooms and tofu, that will leave you feeling nourished.

SERVES 4

Firstly, make the pickled lotus root. Peel and slice the root into 5mm-thick pieces. Mix 1 tablespoon of salt with 300ml of water and use to rinse each slice. Bring a saucepan of water to the boil and add the lotus root. Simmer over a medium heat for 2 minutes. Drain well and place in a bowl with the sushi vinegar. Set aside for at least 6 hours to pickle. This will keep for a couple of days in the fridge.

Soak the shiitake mushrooms in a bowl with 500ml of hot water. Leave for 30 minutes. Drain the shiitake mushrooms (reserving the soaking water) and trim away the stems. Slice the caps into very fine pieces. Cut the hard stems of the shimeji mushrooms off and discard. Break the mushrooms up into bite-sized pieces.

Soak the koya tofu in a bowl with plenty of water to rehydrate for 10 minutes. Drain and gently squeeze any excess water out. Refresh the water and repeat this step a few times. Cut the koya tofu into similar-sized pieces to the carrot.

Put 200ml of the shiitake soaking water, the kombu, sake, soy sauce and sugar in a large pan and bring to the boil over a medium-high heat. Add both kinds of mushrooms, the carrot and koya tofu. Reduce the heat to medium-low and simmer for about 10 minutes, or until the carrot is tender to bite. Remove the pan from the heat and allow the ingredients to cool to room temperature.

Bring a saucepan of salted water to the boil over a high heat. Add the mangetout and blanch for 1 minute, then drain and rinse under cold water to cool completely. Slice finely and set aside.

Drain the mushrooms, carrot and koya tofu from the pan, reserving the cooking liquid. Leave to sit in a colander for 10 minutes.

In a large shallow bowl, mix the sushi rice and all the cooked ingredients together. Add the sesame seeds and combine. If it feels a bit dry, add a little of the reserved cooking liquid. Serve in deep bowls and finish by garnishing with the pickled lotus root slices.

6 dried shiitake mushrooms
80g shimeji mushrooms
2 pieces koya tofu (freeze-dried tofu, available from Asian supermarkets)
1 carrot, peeled and cut into 2cm matchsticks
5g dried kombu
80ml sake
60ml soy sauce
2 tablespoons sugar
50g mangetout or sugar snap peas
450g sushi rice (see page 66)
2 tablespoons toasted sesame seeds
sea salt

FOR THE PICKED LOTUS ROOT
150g lotus root
200ml sushi vinegar

LARGE
PLATES

SHIITAKE OYAKO DONBURI
SHIITAKE AND EGG RICE BOWL

Shiitake mushroom has a beautiful umami flavour, which combined with the soft and creamy texture of eggs makes a perfect topping for a hot steaming bowl of rice.

SERVES 4

Slice away the hard part of the stalks from the mushrooms and slice the caps into 5mm thick pieces.

Heat the dashi stock, soy sauce, mirin, sugar and sake in a wide shallow saucepan over a high heat and add the onion. Simmer for 3 minutes, then add the shiitake mushrooms. Adjust the heat to medium and cook for a further 3 minutes or until the onion becomes transparent.

Meanwhile, beat the eggs in a jug with chopsticks or a fork, making sure not to use a whisk as this will break the natural fibre of the eggs.

When the onion and shiitake mixture is cooked, taste and adjust the flavour – it should be quite intense at this point. Turn the heat up to medium-high and pour the beaten eggs, slowly, into the centre of the pan, using a swirling motion so it reaches the edges of the pan.

Leave the eggs to cook for 1 minute, without mixing. When the eggs look half cooked and still slightly runny, turn off the heat. This will depend on your preference – if you prefer firmer eggs, allow to cook for longer.

Place the freshly cooked piping hot rice in individual bowls. Scoop the egg mixture over the rice and sprinkle with the spring onions. Serve immediately with pickled ginger on top and sansho pepper on the side.

200g shiitake mushrooms
200ml vegetarian dashi stock (see page 166) or ½ teaspoon kombu dashi powder mixed with 200ml hot water
4 tablespoons soy sauce
3 tablespoons mirin
2 tablespoons sugar
1 tablespoon sake
1 large white onion, thinly sliced
6 eggs
600g freshly cooked short-grain rice (see page 168)
2 tablespoons finely chopped spring onions
30g pickled ginger
sansho pepper

TOFU KARAAGE RICE BOWL

We are all familiar with Japanese fried chicken, or chicken *karaage*. I was inspired by the dish and started to play with a few vegetarian versions. When I created this tofu *karaage*, I was so surprised at how tasty it was. You really don't need chicken when tofu does the job this well.

SERVES 4

350g brown short-grain rice
480g firm tofu, cut into 2cm cubes
120g samphire, woody
    parts removed
500ml sunflower or vegetable
    oil, for deep-frying
4 tablespoons cornflour
4 teaspoons seven-spice powder
2 tablespoons toasted ground
    sesame seeds
2 tablespoons black
    sesame seeds

**FOR THE GINGER TERIYAKI
    SAUCE**
90ml soy sauce
60ml mirin
2 tablespoons sugar
1 tablespoon grated ginger
1 teaspoon cornflour

Wash the rice thoroughly in water and leave to soak in 500ml of water in a saucepan for at least 30 minutes or up to 3 hours.

Place the pan over a high heat and bring to the boil. Reduce the heat to the lowest setting and cook for about 30 minutes, covered. Do not stir or keep opening the lid during the cooking as this will release the steam. Once the rice is cooked, turn the heat off and then leave to rest with the lid on for a further 15 minutes.

Mix all the sauce ingredients in a saucepan, except for the cornflour, and bring to the boil over a medium-high heat. Combine the cornflour and 60ml of water in a bowl, then add this to the sauce once it comes up to the boil. Stir well over a medium-low heat, until slightly thickened. Transfer to a large bowl and set aside.

Bring a saucepan of water to the boil and add the tofu cubes. Simmer for about 2 minutes, then use a slotted spoon to transfer the tofu cubes to a colander to drain. Spread the tofu cubes onto a kitchen paper-lined tray and let cool.

Bring the pan back to the boil and add the samphire. (Do not add any salt to the water as samphire is already quite salty.) Blanch for 1 minute, then drain and plunge into ice-cold water. Drain and set aside.

Heat the oil in a wok or large frying pan to 160°C using a thermometer.

Combine the cornflour and seven-spice powder on a large plate. Pat the tofu cubes with kitchen paper and dust with the seasoned cornflour. Add the tofu to the hot oil, in batches, and deep-fry for about 2 minutes or until light golden in colour. Remove with a slotted spoon and drain on kitchen paper. Transfer the tofu straight into the sauce mixture and then gently mix.

Scoop portions of rice into each bowl. Lay the samphire on top of the rice and then sprinkle the ground sesame seeds over. Arrange the tofu cubes on top, then pour over the remaining sauce. Lastly, sprinkle with black sesame seeds.

AUBERGINE AND TOFU RICE BOWL

Aubergine and tofu are like brother and sister. They can both take on strong flavours well and for that reason the two are traditionally used to carry *dengaku*'s heady power.

SERVES 4

Combine the miso with 4 tablespoons of water in a bowl. Add the soy sauce, rice vinegar, sesame oil, grated ginger and sugar, and stir well. Set aside.

Remove and discard the hard woody parts from the samphire. Bring a pan of water to the boil and blanch the samphire for 1 minute. Rinse under cold water until cooled, then set aside in a colander to drain.

Heat the oil for deep-frying in a large frying pan or wok to 170°C.

Mix the cornflour in a bowl with a pinch each of salt and white pepper. Add the aubergine pieces to the bowl and coat in the seasoned cornflour. Place into the hot oil and deep-fry for 2 minutes, turning over frequently until golden brown and the aubergine is cooked. (Do this step in batches.) Drain on kitchen paper.

Heat the remaining 2 tablespoons of oil in a wok or large frying pan and sauté the leek and garlic over a low heat for 2 minutes, until the leek has softened. Increase the heat to medium and then crumble in the tofu. Add half of the sliced chillies and the miso-soy mixture and stir-fry for 2–3 minutes. Stir through the aubergines and samphire, then immediately turn off the heat. Be careful not to cook the aubergines and samphire too long.

Portion out the freshly cooked rice into individual bowls. Place the tofu mixture on top and serve immediately garnished with fresh coriander and the remaining chilli.

30g red miso
4 tablespoons soy sauce
2 tablespoons rice vinegar
2 tablespoons toasted sesame oil
1 tablespoon grated ginger
2 tablespoons caster sugar
80g samphire
1 litre sunflower or vegetable
    oil, for deep-frying, plus
    2 tablespoons
4 tablespoons cornflour
1 large aubergine, cut into large
    bite-sized pieces
1 leek, finely chopped
2 garlic cloves, peeled and
    finely chopped
320g extra firm tofu
2 large red chillies, sliced
600g freshly cooked short-grain
    rice (see page 168)
handful of coriander, chopped,
    to serve
sea salt and ground white pepper

HIJIKI SEAWEED AND EDAMAME RICE BOWL

This colourful and tasty rice dish is super easy to put together. It's a one-pot meal that works any day of the week. Brimming with nutrition, the dish is practically fat free and will leave you feeling virtuous. I love it served with pickled vegetables (see pages 158–166) and miso soup.

SERVES 4

20g hijiki seaweed
300g frozen edamame in pods
100g deep-fried tofu
1 tablespoon vegetable oil
2 carrots, cut into matchsticks
1 teaspoon kombu dashi powder
1 tablespoon sake
1 teaspoon sugar
2 tablespoons mirin
3–4 tablespoons soy sauce
600g freshly cooked
   short-grain brown or white
   rice (see page 168)
sea salt

Soak the hijiki seaweed in a bowl of cold water for about 30 minutes. Rinse under cold running water and drain well in a colander.

Bring plenty of salted water to the boil in a large pan set over a high heat. Add the frozen edamame. Turn the heat down to medium and simmer for about 3 minutes. Rinse under cold water and drain. Pod the beans and set aside.

Pour just-boiled water over the deep-fried tofu sheets in a colander and leave to cool for a few minutes (this step will remove the excess grease). Use clean hands to squeeze any excess water from the tofu sheets, taking care not to tear them. Cut the tofu into 3cm x 1cm strips.

Heat the oil in a large pan over a medium heat and stir-fry the carrots for 2 minutes, or until beginning to soften. Add the hijiki seaweed and then stir-fry for a further 1 minute. Add 60ml of water, the dashi powder, sake, sugar, mirin, soy sauce and the deep-fried tofu to the pan, then stir well. Turn the heat to medium-low and simmer for 4–5 minutes, or until most of the liquid has evaporated.

Add the edamame beans and hijiki mixture to the pan with the cooked rice and combine all the ingredients, taking care not to stir too much as it will make the rice mushy.

SEAWEED

As an island nation, Japan harvests many types of seaweed from all around the country, such as *hijiki* from the crevices of rocks by the sea and kombu from the shallow waters off the coastline. Seaweed has been a central ingredient of Japanese cuisine for thousands of years and is commonplace in both Japanese restaurants and homemade Japanese meals. Healthy, low-calorie, packed with fibre, minerals and flavour, Japanese seaweeds are used in everything from preparing dashi broth, to salads, soups and wrapping sushi rolls. Below are seven of the most commonly used seaweeds.

- **Arame** Usually sold in its dried form, *arame* has dark brown strands and a mild, semi-sweet flavour. Naturally rich in vitamins and minerals it is also highly beneficial to the skin.

- **Hijiki** Collected from the rocky coastlines of Japan, *hijiki* has a thin and knobby (somewhat branch-like appearance) and a nutty, earthy and slightly fishy flavour. It is commonly added to stews and soups, but also shines in salads when combined with fried tofu, carrots, edamame and other fresh vegetables and dressed with sweetened soy sauce, and mirin. *Hijiki* is purchased in its dried form, and is rehydrated in water before use.

- **Kanten (agar agar)** A jellifying agent extracted from seaweed. It's typically used for making puddings, custards and *wagashi*, a traditional Japanese sweet. It is an excellent plant-based alternative to gelatine derived from animal products. It can be bought in powdered, stick, thread and flaked form, and is dissolved in water then boiled before use.

- **Kombu** Sea kelp is an important ingredient and used to make dashi, the basic stock for practically all Japanese recipes. It has a tough, leathery texture and must be rehydrated before use. Packed with calcium and iron and with a savoury umami flavour, in addition to being used in broths, kombu can be cooked in a *tsukudani* style, similar to a chutney, or used to prepare kombucha. I use kombu as a background flavour for many slow-cooked dishes as it imparts a deep natural sweetness and saltiness.

- **Nori** Perhaps the most familiar seaweed to people outside of Japan, nori is almost always eaten dried and is sold in sheets or strips for making sushi or for eating as a snack. Dried nori sheets are produced by pressing shredded edible red algae into thin sheets and drying them. Other forms of nori include *kizami nori* (shredded nori), for garnishing dishes such as rice bowls, and ao-nori (seaweed) powder, used as a condiment. *Ajitsuke nori* (flavoured nori) is also available, with common flavourings including soy sauce, sugar and sesame oil.

- **Mozuku** A brown seaweed that is the pride of Okinawa, and rarely found outside of Japan. Ninety nine per cent of the world's production is made in the southern archipelago of Japan, known for being the place with the longest human life expectancy. Whilst all seaweeds are packed with nutrients, *mozuku* has the most nutritional value of all and is said to help improve blood circulation and promote fat loss.

- **Wakame** This is one of the most commonly consumed types of seaweed in Japan, boasting a mild, sweet flavour. Fresh wakame is harvested from the Sea of Japan from February to June, but dried wakame is available year-round and can be easily reconstituted by soaking in water. Wakame is a common addition to salads, pickled vegetables and miso soup.

TURNIP LEAF RISOTTO

This is one of my most successful creations. The slight bitterness from the turnip leaves gives the dish a sensational taste, and creates such harmony with the rich and sweet egg yolk. For this recipe, it is an absolute must to use the best-quality eggs you can find.

SERVES 4

Wash the turnip leaves and stalks thoroughly, then trim away and discard the bottom part of the stalks. Finely chop the leaves and stalks. Cut the base of the enoki mushrooms and separate into clumps.

Heat the oil in a large pan over a medium heat and add the rice. Fry for 1 minute and then add the sake. Allow the alcohol to cook off for about 30 seconds, stirring the rice at all times.

Put the stock into a jug or similar vessel. Add about 200ml of the stock to the pan and reduce the heat to medium-low. Continue to cook and stir for about 3 minutes, or until the liquid has been absorbed by the rice. Repeat with another 200ml of the stock, stirring until the liquid has been absorbed by the rice. If you find the liquid is being absorbed rapidly, reduce the heat to low. Repeat once more, then add the chopped turnip leaves and stalks and continue stirring. Add the remaining stock in this way until it is used and the rice is cooked. When the rice is cooked, add the miso, soy sauce and salt, stirring to combine. Stir through the enoki mushrooms and continue to cook for another 3 minutes.

Bring a saucepan of water to the boil with the rice vinegar over a medium-high heat. Crack 2 eggs into the water. Turn the heat down to medium and then cook for 2 minutes. Take the eggs out using a slotted spoon and drain on kitchen paper. Repeat for the remaining 2 eggs.

For the risotto, turn off the heat when most of the liquid has absorbed but it is still very wet and creamy. Spoon the rice into shallow bowls and then top with the poached eggs. Sprinkle over the deep-fried shallots and serve.

240g turnip leaves, including stalks
120g enoki mushrooms
3 tablespoons sunflower or vegetable oil
450g white short-grain rice
60ml sake
1 litre vegetarian dashi stock (see page 166), or 2 teaspoons kombu dashi powder mixed with 1 litre hot water
80g white miso
1 tablespoon soy sauce
½ teaspoon sea salt
1 tablespoon rice vinegar
4 free-range organic eggs
4 tablespoons deep-fried shallots

TIP
This is also delicious using Swiss chard as an alternative to turnip leaf.

NOZAWANA-ZUKE
PICKLED SWISS CHARD AND EGG FRIED RICE

Nozawana-zuke are preserved mustard greens, which are popular in Japan as a side or mixed into various dishes. I set myself the challenge of using Swiss chard instead of mustard greens and it has lead to this success. It takes a bit of preparation but it's worth a try. I think it's simply delicious with plain rice or noodles.

SERVES 4

3 tablespoons sunflower
   or vegetable oil
4 eggs
700g freshly cooked short-grain
   rice (see page 168)
½ teaspoon ground
   white pepper
2 tablespoons toasted sesame
   seeds, plus extra to serve
sea salt

FOR THE PICKLED
SWISS CHARD
500g Swiss chard
120ml rice vinegar
2 tablespoons sunflower or
   vegetable oil
1 or 2 red chillies, thinly sliced
4 tablespoons soy sauce
4 tablespoons mirin
2 tablespoons sesame oil

To prepare the Swiss chard, trim the base of the chard and separate the stalks. Wash them thoroughly. Slice the stalks and green leaves into 5cm chunks and set aside.

In a large pan, bring 2 litres of water to the boil over a medium-high heat. Add the rice vinegar and blanch the stalks for 4–5 minutes, then add the leaves and simmer together for 2 more minutes. Drain and rinse under cold water and then squeeze any excess water out. Chop the leaves and stalks into 1cm-thick pieces.

Heat the oil in a large frying pan or wok and add the pickled Swiss chard to the pan. Add the chillies, soy sauce and mirin, and stir-fry over a medium heat for 3–4 minutes, or until most of the liquid evaporates. Add the sesame oil and fry for a further 1 minute. Take off the heat and leave to cool. At this stage, the pickle can be stored in a clean container in the fridge for 4–5 days.

Heat 1 tablespoon of the oil in a large frying pan or wok over a medium heat and then crack in the eggs. Add a pinch of salt and stir quickly, scrambling the eggs until just cooked. Immediately take off the heat and remove to a plate.

Add the remaining 2 tablespoons of oil and cooked rice to the pan with a pinch of salt and the white pepper. Stir-fry the rice for 2–3 minutes, over a medium heat, breaking up the lumps, then return the eggs to the pan and add the pickled Swiss chard and sesame seeds. Cook for a further 2 minutes, mixing well.

Serve in bowls and garnish with extra sesame seeds.

TIP

The recipe here is for a quick pickle but if you have time, blanch the chard in the water only, and mix the rice vinegar with 1 teaspoon each of sugar, salt and Dijon mustard in a glass bowl. Add the Swiss chard, mixing well. Cover with clingfilm and place a weight on top. Leave to pickle for 24 hours in a cool place but not in the fridge, turning the Swiss chard a couple of times.

OMU RICE

Omu is short for omelette, so this dish is simply rice with omelette on top. It is one of the classic fusion dishes that are traditional and have been eaten casually around the Japanese table for a long time.

For this recipe, it is better to use the rice from the day before and keep it in the fridge overnight rather than freshly cooked as that would be too wet.

Heat 40ml of the oil in a large wok or frying pan over a medium heat and add the onion, garlic, pepper and carrot. Stir-fry for about 3 minutes, and then add the mushrooms and sausage or tofu, and cook for a further 3 minutes.

Add another 40ml of the oil and the rice to the wok and use a wooden spatula to spread the rice out in the wok, pressing it down. Stir-fry by scooping the rice from the bottom and using a turning and flipping motion. Cook for about 1 minute and season with a little salt, pepper and chilli if you like. Stir in the tomato purée, ketchup, tonkatsu sauce and soy sauce, and cook for a further 2 minutes. Turn off the heat and leave the rice in the wok to keep warm.

Whisk the eggs in a large bowl. Heat a non-stick frying pan over a high heat and add 1 teaspoon of oil along with about a quarter of the butter. Once the pan is very hot, pour a quarter of the egg mixture into the pan and then scramble the centre a little by shaking a pan. As soon as the egg is just about cooked yet still runny, turn off the heat.

Tip a quarter of the rice mixture on top of the egg and spread out evenly over the surface. Let it warm through for a few minutes, then carefully flip out on to a plate.

Repeat for the remaining rice and egg and serve in individual bowls. Mix together the tonkatsu sauce and tomato ketchup in a bowl, then dollop on top of the rice and egg.

SERVES 4

100ml sunflower or vegetable oil
1 onion, finely chopped
2 garlic cloves, finely chopped
1 green pepper, cored and finely chopped
1 large carrot, peeled and finely chopped
120g chestnut mushrooms, diced
4 vegetarian sausages or 160g smoked tofu, cut into bite-sized pieces
600g cooked short-grain rice (see page 168), see recipe introduction
½ teaspoon ground white pepper
½ dried chilli, flaked, optional
1 tablespoon tomato purée
2 tablespoons tomato ketchup
2 tablespoons tonkatsu sauce (see page 168), or tomato ketchup or Worcestershire sauce
2 tablespoons soy sauce
6 large eggs or 8 medium eggs
20g butter
sea salt

TO SERVE
100ml tonkatsu sauce (see page 168) or Worcestershire sauce
100ml tomato ketchup

EGG AND HIJIKI SOUFFLÉ

This may look like an ordinary cheese soufflé, but don't be fooled. The flavour is completely Japanese, and in fact, very similar to traditional steamed egg custard (*chawanmushi*). It's so light, fluffy and easy to devour.

SERVES 4

6g dried hijiki seaweed
2 tablespoons soy sauce
1 tablespoon mirin
80ml vegetarian dashi stock
  (see page 166)
1½ teaspoons sake
4 eggs
½ teaspoon sugar
¼ teaspoon shichimi pepper
small handful of watercress,
  roughly chopped
sea salt

Soak the hijiki seaweed in a bowl of warm water for at least 10 minutes. Drain away the water, leaving a little behind and place in a small saucepan with 1 tablespoon of soy sauce and the mirin. Heat gently for 2–3 minutes, making sure the cooking liquid does not evaporate completely. Turn off the heat and leave to sit.

Preheat the oven to 180°C/160°C fan/gas mark 4.

Heat the dashi stock with the remaining 1 tablespoon of soy sauce, sake and a pinch of salt in a saucepan for 2–3 minutes over a medium heat.

Divide the dashi broth between 4 individual ramekins about 150ml in capacity. Divide the seaweed between the ramekins.

Meanwhile, separate the eggs, making sure to put the whites into a very clean large bowl. Add the sugar and ¼ teaspoon of salt and, using an electric mixer or hand whisk, beat until the egg whites are fluffy and stiff enough to form soft peaks.

Mix the egg yolks with the hijiki mixture and season with the shichimi pepper. Add the egg whites to the egg yolk mixture and fold very gently until combined.

Scoop the soufflé mixture into the individual ramekins and cook in the oven for 10–12 minutes.

Remove the soufflés from the oven and garnish with the roughly chopped watercress. Serve immediately.

OKONOMIYAKI
KIMCHI AND CHEDDAR CHEESE SAVOURY PANCAKE

Okonomiyaki is an icon of Japanese street cooking, and for me the quintessential comfort food. A savoury pancake that can contain an array of ingredients, the name translates as 'how you like' or 'what you like'. The smell of *okonomiyaki* being cooked is something else, it's mouth-watering, and the taste addictive.

SERVES 4

In a large bowl, mix the flour with the dashi powder and 750ml of water. Once combined, add the beaten eggs and baking powder then mix well until the batter is smooth.

Remove the thick ribs from the cabbage leaves and slice the leaves thinly. Add to the batter along with the spring onions.

Heat ½ tablespoon of the oil in a frying pan over a medium heat. Spoon in a quarter of the cabbage mixture, flatten with a spatula to help spread the batter evenly across the pan (you are aiming for a thickness of about 1.5cm–2cm), and then turn the heat down to very low and fry for 3 minutes.

Lay some of the kimchi over the top of the pancake. Partially cover with a lid (to release the condensation) and cook for about 7–8 minutes (depending on the size of the pancake), making sure the bottom of the pancake is crisp but not burnt. Sprinkle over a little grated cheese, then flip over and cook for a further 3–4 minutes, uncovered.

Flip the pancake over again and cook for a further 1 minute, then transfer to a plate. Repeat with the remaining 3 pancakes.

To serve, drizzle the tonkatsu sauce over the pancakes using a knife to help spread it out evenly on the surface. Do the same with the mayonnaise if you wish. Sprinkle with the ao-nori powder and deep-fried shallots and serve immediately with mustard on the side.

375g plain flour
3 teaspoons kombu dashi powder
3 eggs, lightly beaten
½ teaspoon baking powder
1 head of pointed cabbage
bunch of spring onions, finely chopped
2 tablespoons vegetable oil
160g kimchi
160g Cheddar cheese, or other hard cheese of choice, grated
tonkatsu sauce (see page 168 or use shop-bought)
Japanese mayonnaise (see page 167) or shop-bought mayonnaise, optional
2 tablespoons ao-nori (seaweed) powder
4 tablespoons deep-fried shallots
Japanese mustard or Dijon mustard, to serve

GREEN TEA SOBA
WITH SHIITAKE AND CORN TEMPURA

Tempura soba is extremely popular in Japan. It's versatile and variations abound. With this version of the dish you get to enjoy the tempura batter in a different way as it becomes creamy as opposed to crispy. *Cha soba* is a buckwheat noodle (*soba*) infused with green tea. It makes the dish pretty, but feel free to substitute ordinary soba noodles.

SERVES 4

2 litres vegetarian dashi
  stock (see page 166) or
  1 tablespoon kombu dashi
  powder mixed with 2 litres
  hot water
80ml soy sauce
60ml mirin
4 tablespoons sake
1 teaspoon salt
120g shiitake mushrooms
200g tempura flour
approx. 250ml ice-cold water
4 baby corn, cut into small pieces
1 litre sunflower or vegetable oil,
  for deep-frying
320g dried cha soba
  noodles or ordinary soba
  (buckwheat) noodles
80g daikon radish, grated, plus
  a little extra to garnish
50g ginger, peeled and grated,
  plus a little extra to garnish

Bring the dashi stock to the boil over a medium-high heat in a saucepan. When it comes to the boil, add the soy sauce, mirin, sake and salt, and then simmer over a low heat for about 10 minutes.

While simmering the broth, remove the tough stalks from the mushrooms and then chop the caps into cubes.

Put the tempura flour in a bowl and then add the cold water and roughly mix to make a batter. Add the chopped mushrooms and baby corn to the batter, and then mix, making sure the vegetables are evenly covered in the batter.

Heat the oil in a wide deep-frying pan or wok to 160°C using a thermometer. Alternatively, check the temperature of the oil by dropping a little batter into the oil. If the batter stays in the bottom of the pan for more than 2 seconds, then the temperature is too low. If the batter floats up immediately and oil spits, then the temperature is too high. At the right temperature, the batter should touch the bottom of the pan then immediately come up naturally to the top without oil spluttering.

When the oil is ready, take a tablespoon of the vegetable batter and drop into the hot oil. Be careful not to overcrowd the pan. (It is best to fry in batches.) Fry for about 2 minutes, until light golden all over. Remove with a slotted spoon and drain on kitchen paper.

Bring a large pan of salted water to the boil and add the soba noodles. Cook for 4–5 minutes or following the packet instructions. Drain.

Meanwhile, reheat the broth and bring back to the boil. Squeeze any excess water out from the grated daikon and add to the broth along with the ginger.

Divide the noodles between 4 individual bowls and then pour over the broth. Arrange 2 or 3 pieces of tempura on top. Serve the noodles with side bowls of extra daikon and ginger so each person can add their own to their liking.

YASAI YAKISOBA
COLOURFUL VEGETABLE YAKISOBA

The smell of tonkatsu sauce cooking for *yakisoba* is the classic calling card of Japanese street food. It draws you in. The dish itself is a kind of noodle stir-fry, and it's eaten both on the street and as a casual office lunch.

SERVES 4

Bring a pan of water to the boil and cook the noodles for 6 minutes, until just tender.

Heat 2 tablespoons of the oil in a wok over a medium heat and stir-fry the leek and garlic for 1 minute. Add the tofu, remaining vegetables and soy sauce, and stir-fry for 2–3 minutes.

Add the cooked noodles to the wok, turn up the heat to high and season with the salt and pepper. Stir-fry for a further 2–3 minutes. Stir in the tonkatsu sauce, and then cook for a further 1 minute. Turn off the heat.

Divide the noodles between individual plates or bowls. Sprinkle with the deep-fried shallots and ao-nori powder and serve immediately.

400g dried egg noodles
4 tablespoons sunflower or
  vegetable oil
1 leek, finely sliced
2 garlic cloves, peeled and
  finely sliced
240g smoked tofu, diced into
  bite-sized pieces
4 large shiitake mushrooms, cut
  into bite-sized pieces
1 green pepper, cored and sliced
  into 5cm-long strips
1 red pepper, cored and sliced
  into 5cm-long strips
1 yellow pepper, cored and
  sliced into 5cm-long strips
1 tablespoon soy sauce
1 teaspoon sea salt
½ teaspoon ground
  white pepper
200ml tonkatsu sauce
  (see page 168)
6 tablespoons deep-fried
  shallots, to serve
4 tablespoons ao-nori
  (seaweed) powder, to serve

SOBA NOODLES
WITH MISO SPINACH PESTO

Mixing spinach, pine nuts and miso together makes for a perfect, rich Japanese pesto. The nuttiness of the soba noodles goes so well with the miso pesto, and the whole dish is utterly delicious!

SERVES 4

400g spinach leaves
50g toasted pine nuts
120ml olive oil
50g miso paste
4 tablespoons mirin
50g ginger, grated
1 clove garlic, grated
2 large red chillies, or ½ red
    pepper, finely chopped
320g dried soba noodles
sea salt

To make spinach pesto, bring a large pan of salted water to the boil over a high heat. Add the spinach leaves and cook for 30–40 seconds. Rinse under cold running water until the spinach is cold. Drain well and then gently squeeze out any remaining water, leaving a little moisture in the spinach.

Add the drained spinach, toasted pine nuts, olive oil, miso paste, mirin, ginger and garlic to a food processor, along with some good-quality sea salt, and then blitz for about 1 minute. Don't over-blitz, but ensure there is a little bit of texture in the pesto. Remove to a bowl and stir in the chilli, or red pepper.

Cook the soba noodles until they are al dente, according to the packet instructions. Rinse them under hot running water and then put the noodles and pesto back in the saucepan used to cook the noodles and heat them together for 30 seconds. If it becomes too dry, add a little more olive oil to taste.

Divide the noodles between 4 individual bowls and serve.

TIP
Do not add the red chilli or pepper into the food processor as they will be blended into the spinach mixture and change the pesto flavour and colour.

AUBERGINE AND PADRÓN PEPPER
WITH SOMEN NOODLES

This noodle dish is a love letter to aubergines and little green padrón peppers. It's super simple but is among my very favourite recipes. You must try it. The dish can also be served cold. To do so, allow the broth and vegetables to cool down first, and drain the cooked noodles under cold water.

SERVES 4

Put the dashi stock, soy sauce, mirin, sake and a pinch of salt into a large pan and cook for 5–6 minutes. Turn off the heat and set aside in the pan. If you are serving the dish cold (see recipe introduction), cool the broth and then keep in the fridge until required.

To prepare the aubergines, trim away the top part and then cut the aubergines in half. Cut each piece vertically into 2.5cm-wide and 7cm-long wedges.

Heat the oil in a wok or large frying pan to 170°C. Add the peppers to the hot oil, in batches, and deep-fry for about 2 minutes, depending on their size. Remove with a slotted spoon and drain on kitchen paper.

Add the aubergines to the oil, again in batches, and deep-fry for 2 minutes, moving them often, until golden brown. Remove with a slotted spoon and drain on kitchen paper.

Bring a large pan of water to the boil and cook the noodles for 2–3 minutes. Rinse under cold water and drain.

Meanwhile, reheat the broth (if serving hot) in the pan. As soon as the noodles are cooked, add to the simmering broth and turn off the heat.

Divide the noodles between 4 large soup bowls. Pour over the broth and then arrange the aubergines and peppers on top. Finish the dish with the grated ginger and finely chopped spring onions and serve immediately.

1 litre vegetarian dashi stock (see page 166) or 2 teaspoons kombu dashi powder mixed with 1 litre hot water
60ml soy sauce
60ml mirin
20ml sake
2 large aubergines
1.5 litres sunflower or vegetable oil, for deep-frying
16–20 padrón peppers
400g dried somen noodles or soba (buckwheat) noodles
4 tablespoons grated ginger, to serve
2 spring onions, finely chopped, or small bunch of coriander, to serve
sea salt

SOBA LEI MEN
SOBA SALAD WITH SMOKED TOFU AND AVOCADO

This is a super fresh noodle dish that can be eaten as a refreshing summer lunch. You can add other vegetables as you like.

SERVES 4

300g dried soba (buckwheat)
   noodles
1 cucumber
1 large yellow pepper
1 avocado
60g samphire, woody
   bits removed
1 tablespoon vegetable or
   sunflower oil
2 tablespoons toasted
   sesame seeds
200g smoked tofu or/and
   vegetarian sausage, cut
   into thin pieces
sea salt

FOR THE DRESSING
80ml soy sauce
60ml rice vinegar
4 tablespoons mirin
1 tablespoon sugar
2 tablespoons sesame oil
3 tablespoons grated ginger
4 tablespoons sesame seeds,
   toasted and ground

Break the soba noodles in half to shorten. Bring a large pan of water to the boil and add the noodles. Cook over a medium heat according to the packet, around 3 minutes, until tender. Drain and rinse under cold water. Leave in the colander to drain completely.

Trim both ends of the cucumber, then peel and cut in half lengthways. Remove the seeds, then slice on the diagonal into thin long pieces. Remove the core and seeds from the pepper and slice thinly to match the cucumber. Halve the avocado, remove the stone and cut the flesh into thin segments.

Bring a small pan of salted water to the boil and blanch the samphire for 1 minute. Drain and set aside.

Add the vegetable or sunflower oil to a small frying pan and, once hot, sauté the samphire for 1–2 minutes. Add the sesame seeds, mix together and move from the heat.

Portion the noodles out into individual plates or shallow bowls. Place each ingredient on top of the noodles, making sure to keep them separate. For example, start with the cucumber, then the pepper, then the avocado, then the tofu and/or sausages.

Mix all the ingredients for the dressing in a bowl and then pour the dressing into 4 small bowls. Place the samphire in the middle of all the toppings and then serve with the dressing on the side.

KITSUNE UDON

The word *kitsune* means 'fox' in Japanese, but in cooking acts as a nickname for deep-fried tofu. I think it's because of the russet-brown colour, but in Japanese folklore foxes are thought to have a taste for tofu. Typically tofu is cut into a triangular shape so it looks like a fox. Here the fox loves udon noodles.

SERVES 4

To prepare the tofu, slice the block in half and wrap in kitchen paper. Press between 2 chopping boards with a weight (such as a tin of beans) on the top. Arrange in the sink on a slight angle, so that excess water can drain away. Leave for 1–2 hours.

Remove the tofu from the boards and kitchen paper. Cut into slices about 1cm thick.

Heat the oil in a wok or large frying pan to 160°C.

Pat each tofu slice with kitchen paper to soak up any excess moisture. Carefully add to the hot oil, in batches if necessary, and deep-fry for 2–3 minutes, or until golden brown all over. Repeat until all the slices are used. Remove with a slotted spoon and drain on kitchen paper.

Next, pour 500ml of water into a large pan along with the shiitake mushrooms, soy sauce, sake and sugar. Add the deep-fried tofu, bring to the boil over a high heat, reduce the heat to medium-low and cook, covered, for 10–12 minutes. Make sure to turn the tofu slices over and baste with the liquid a few times during this time. Take off the heat and allow the tofu to cool in the pan. Once cooled, remove the tofu from the broth and cut into triangles.

Trim the bottom hard parts off the enoki mushrooms and separate the stems. Remove the shiitake mushrooms from the pan and slice into pieces 5mm–7mm thick.

Add the dashi stock to the mushroom broth in the pan and set over a medium heat. Add the spring onions and enoki mushrooms and simmer for about 2 minutes. In the meantime, prepare and cook the noodles in a separate pan, according to the packet instructions, and drain.

Divide the udon noodles between large soup bowls. Place the deep-fried tofu triangles on top. Pour the broth over the noodles and add the spring onions and all the mushrooms.

Serve immediately with grated ginger and shichimi pepper on the side.

400g firm tofu
700ml sunflower or vegetable oil, for deep-frying
2 dried shiitake mushrooms
80ml soy sauce
60ml sake
2 tablespoons sugar
200g enoki mushrooms
2 litres vegetarian dashi stock (see page 166), or 3 teaspoons kombu dashi powder mixed with 2 litres hot water
2 bunches of spring onions, cut on the diagonal into 5mm thick slices
400g udon noodles
2 tablespoons grated ginger, to serve
shichimi pepper, to serve

SOY AND GINGER YAKI-UDON

The addition of soy sauce and ginger creates a signature flavour of Japanese cooking. All the ingredients used for this authentic dish can be obtained from your local supermarket.

SERVES 4

400g dried udon noodles
2 tablespoons sunflower or
   vegetable oil
1 white onion, thinly sliced
2 garlic cloves, finely chopped
2 teaspoons finely grated ginger
2 red large chillies, deseeded
   and finely chopped
2 small courgettes, finely sliced
2 carrots, sliced into long and
   very thin ribbons using a
   mandoline or vegetable peeler
80g shiitake mushrooms,
   stalks removed and caps
   finely chopped
½ teaspoon ground
   white pepper
2 nori sheets, torn into
   small pieces
2 spring onions, finely chopped

FOR THE SOY AND
   GINGER SAUCE
2 tablespoons grated ginger
80ml mirin
80ml soy sauce
2 tablespoons toasted sesame oil

Simply boil the noodles in a pan of water for 10 minutes, then drain well.

Mix all the ingredients for the soy and ginger sauce in a bowl and set aside.

Heat the oil in a large wok of frying pan and add the onion, garlic and ginger and stir-fry for 1 minute, over a medium-high heat. Stir in the chillies, courgettes, carrots and mushrooms and sauté over a medium-low heat for 2–3 minutes. Add the noodles and stir-fry for another 2 minutes, turn up the heat and pour in the soy ginger sauce and continue to cook for a further minute. Season with the pepper, then turn off the heat and divide the noodles and veg between individual bowls.

Sprinkle over the nori and finely chopped spring onions and serve.

MISO RAMEN

For this vegetarian ramen I've used plenty of kombu and dried shiitake mushrooms, which provide the deep and powerful flavour to the broth. I think it definitely gives the traditional meaty ramen a run for its money.

SERVES 4

Put all the ingredients for the broth in a large pan with 6 litres of water and bring to the boil over a high heat. Turn down the heat to medium-low and simmer for 2–3 hours, checking the water and topping up at all times. (You may cook this in a pressure cooker for 30–40 minutes, making sure the water level is at maximum level when you start.)

Remove from the heat and drain the broth into a large bowl, then return to the pan. Set over a high heat and bring to the boil, then add the seasonings. Turn down the heat to low and simmer for 3 minutes.

To cook fresh noodles, bring a large pan of water to the boil and add the noodles. Cook for 2–3 minutes, depending on the thickness of the noodles. For dried noodles, cook according to the packet instructions. Drain and set aside.

Meanwhile, if using, cook the eggs for the topping. Put the eggs in a small pan of water and bring to the boil; cook for 4–5 minutes after the water comes to the boil for soft-boiled egg or a minute or two longer if you prefer hard-boiled egg. Remove and plunge in cold water. Peel when cool enough to handle.

To prepare the rest of the toppings, blanch the baby corn and sugar snap peas in a small pan of boiling water for 2 minutes. Remove and rinse under cold water. Drain well. Heat a dash of oil in a frying pan over a medium-high heat and stir-fry the vegetarian sausages for 2 minutes. Add the baby corn and sugar snap peas and stir-fry for a minute, then add the shiitake mushrooms and bamboo shoots. Toss well for a minute or until the vegetables are just cooked.

To serve, add a couple of ladlefuls of broth to each serving bowl. Portion the noodles out into each bowl. Arrange your choice of toppings over the noodles. Serve immediately with chilli sauce and a little extra white pepper if you like.

560–640g fresh ramen noodles or 400g dried noodles
chilli sauce, optional

FOR THE BROTH
80g ginger, peeled and roughly sliced
2 leeks, roughly chopped
2 large onions, quartered
4 carrots, quartered
1 cabbage core (the part normally not used)
10–15g dried kombu
6 dried shiitake mushrooms
10–15 black peppercorns
250ml sake

FOR THE SEASONINGS
2 tablespoons sake
4 tablespoons soy sauce
3 tablespoons miso
4 tablespoons ground toasted sesame seeds
sea salt and ground white pepper

FOR THE TOPPINGS – AS MUCH AS YOU LIKE AND CHOICE OF ANY
soft-boiled eggs
baby corn
sugar snap peas
vegetarian sausages, cut into bite-sized pieces
shiitake mushrooms, thinly sliced
pickled bamboo shoots
silken tofu, cut into 2cm cubes

SILKEN TOFU AND MUSHROOMS IN BROTH

This is a lovely, subtle, clean-tasting and light dish. Using the finest quality tofu is of the utmost importance here as it is the star of the show.

SERVES 4

120g shiitake mushrooms
120g enoki mushrooms
100g mangetout
1 litre vegetarian dashi stock
    (see page 166), or 3
    teaspoons kombu dashi
    powder mixed with 1 litre
    hot water
60ml sake
40ml mirin
60ml soy sauce
600g silken tofu, cut into
    bite-sized cubes
2 tablespoons cornflour mixed
    with 60ml water
80g grated ginger, plus extra
    to serve
shichimi pepper, to serve
sea salt

Take the stalks off the shiitake mushrooms and cut the caps into about 5mm slices. Cut off the bottom hard part of the enoki mushrooms and cut the top part in half lengthways, and break apart.

Blanch the mangetout in a pan of boiling salted water for 1 minute. Drain under cold water and leave in a colander.

Heat the dashi stock in a large pan, add the sake, mirin and soy sauce, and bring to the boil. Add the mushrooms and tofu, and simmer over a low heat for 5–6 minutes. Increase the heat to high and add the cornflour mixture to the pan. Bring back up to the boil, and allow to simmer for a couple of minutes until thickened. Turn off the heat.

Immediately add the blanched mangetout and grated ginger to the broth and stir gently. Divide between shallow serving bowls, making sure to distribute the ingredients evenly. Serve the extra grated ginger and shichimi pepper on the side.

SUKIYAKI HOTPOT

Sukiyaki without beef? Indeed. It's my yummy veg version of this traditional *nabe* (hotpot). It's so light, and the teriyaki flavour is always so moreish. Using raw egg as a dipping sauce may push you out of your comfort zone, but give it a try. Just make sure to use the best-quality and freshest eggs you can find.

SERVES 4

Heat a large casserole dish, Japanese *nabe* (hotpot) or large deep frying pan with the oil. Add the leeks, onion, ginger and carrots to the pan and sauté over a medium-high heat for about 3 minutes, or until the vegetables are softened. Pour in 480ml of water and add the kombu dashi powder, then bring to the boil over a high heat.

As soon as it comes to boil, add the soy sauce, mirin, sake and sugar and stir well. Keeping each component separate in the pan, add the white part of the Chinese cabbage, the mushrooms, the tofu and the shirataki noodles. Cover with a lid and cook for 3–4 minutes over a medium heat.

Add the remaining green part of the cabbage to the pan, making sure the vegetables are immersed in the broth. Put the lid back on and cook for a further 2 minutes.

Serve the casserole on the table or scoop portions out into individual bowls. Serve with the eggs as a dipping sauce and with the sansho pepper on the side.

4 tablespoons sunflower or
  vegetable oil
2 leeks, thinly sliced
1 onion, finely diced
40g ginger, peeled and sliced
  (preferably slice against the
  fibre as this allows it to release
  more flavour)
2 carrots, peeled and thinly sliced
  on the diagonal
2 tablespoons kombu
  dashi powder
120ml soy sauce
80ml mirin
4 tablespoons sake
2–3 tablespoons sugar
1 Chinese cabbage, cut into
  2.5cm-thick slices, white and
  green parts separated
8 large shiitake mushrooms,
  halved
400g firm tofu, cut into
  2cm cubes
400g shirataki noodles
4 eggs, lightly beaten, optional
sansho pepper, to serve

MUSHROOM HOTPOT FEAST

There is a huge variety of mushrooms that are eaten in Japan and likewise an array of *nabe*, hotpot dishes. I've brought these two popular foods together in a dish that is all about the convivial spirit, one that is to be made and eaten at the table among friends and family. If at all possible, cook the hotpot on the table over a camping burner.

The rice and egg is served like a second course. After you have finished feasting on the vegetables and mushrooms you whisk the eggs and rice into the pot, soaking up the remnants of flavour. You can use ponzu dipping sauce or extra soy sauce to season your portion as you like, and you could use udon or somen noodles instead of rice.

SERVES 4

250g enoki mushrooms
250g shimeji mushrooms
250g shiitake mushrooms,
  stalks removed
1 litre vegetarian dashi stock
  (see page 166) or 2 teaspoons
  kombu dashi powder mixed
  with 1 litre hot water
1 large Chinese cabbage, white
  and green parts separated,
  roughly sliced
2 leeks, white and green
  parts separated, cut into
  1cm thick rounds
100g watercress,
  roughly chopped
2 tablespoons sake
2 tablespoons mirin
2 tablespoons soy sauce
4 eggs
600g freshly cooked short-grain
  rice (see page 168)
2 spring onions, finely chopped,
  or a few chopped chive stalks
sea salt and ground white pepper

FOR THE PONZU DIPPING SAUCE
125ml soy sauce
100ml rice vinegar
60ml mirin
2 tablespoons lemon or lime juice
1–2 tablespoons sugar
1 onion, grated

Prepare the mushrooms by using a sheet of damp kitchen paper to wipe off any soil. For the enoki and shimeji mushrooms, cut away the base. If the shiitake mushrooms are large, cut them in half.

Set the table up with the burner (see recipe introduction) and serving bowls. Heat the dashi stock in a hotpot-style dish, casserole dish or wide and shallow saucepan over the burner and bring to the boil over a medium-high heat.

Add half of the white part of the Chinese cabbage and leek. Simmer over a medium heat for about 2 minutes, then add about a quarter of each kind of mushroom, the green parts of the Chinese cabbage and the watercress. Simmer for another 2 minutes or until the mushrooms are just cooked. Season to taste.

In 2 separate bowls, mix together the dipping sauces. I like to divide the dipping sauces into separate small bowls for each person but this is not altogether necessary. Guests can help themselves to the dipping sauces.

When you are ready to eat, gradually add the remaining mushrooms and vegetables, and cook as you and your diners eat.

Once all the mushrooms and vegetables have been cooked and eaten, quickly whisk the eggs in a small bowl. Turn up the heat to high and add the rice. Pour the whisked eggs over the rice and cook for 30 seconds. Immediately turn off the heat. Sprinkle the finely chopped spring onions or chives over the top and eat.

TIP

You can use any type of
mushrooms for this recipe,
although I recommend selecting
a variety of textures so you can
enjoy soft and juicy mushrooms,
as well as the crunch and meaty
flavour of others.

**FOR THE SESAME
  DIPPING SAUCE**

4 tablespoons tahini
6 tablespoons ground toasted
  sesame seeds
80ml soy sauce
50ml mirin
50ml rice vinegar
2 tablespoons sugar

JAPANESE MUSHROOMS

A wide variety of foods make up the well-balanced Japanese diet, or *washoku*, and while many people are aware of the benefits of tofu, seaweed and green tea, fewer are aware of Japanese mushrooms, which are delicious and flavourful. Below are seven types of Japanese mushrooms eaten daily.

- **Enoki** Delicate, white, long and slender, enoki mushrooms are almost as popular as shiitake. The variety most commonly available in the West is creamy white, with stems as thin as soba or ramen noodles and round caps no bigger than 1.5cm in diameter. While they don't have much flavour of their own, they absorb the flavours they are cooked in extremely well. Their distinctive shape and texture is used to add interest to dishes.

- **Eryngii (trumpet mushroom)** After discovering these somewhat sexy-looking mushrooms a few years ago, they've become my favourite variety. What really stands out is not the flavour, which is rather plain, but the texture: meaty and juicy, with just the right amount of resistance to the bite. The best way to enjoy them is simply braised, highlighting their wonderful texture.

- **Maitake** The name comes from the word 'dancing', which aptly describes the appearance of this delicate and frilly mushroom. The undulating wavy brown caps grow en masse out of clumps of white stems, somewhat resembling oyster mushrooms. The soft, moist texture and dense, woody flavour is best enjoyed sautéed or used in clear broths. Maitake can be found at Japanese grocery stores.

- **Matsutake** Known as the king of mushrooms for their superb, earthy and intense flavour, matsutake mushrooms are found only in the wild. Prized for their ability to infuse their distinctive aroma to anything they touch, they are the most expensive variety of mushroom, often costing around £60–£70 per kilo. More recently, matsutake have been imported from countries such as China, Korea, Morocco and Turkey, increasing their availability and lowering the price to within reach of the average person.

- **Nameko** Perhaps the most unknown on this list and hard to find outside of Japan, this mushroom has a slimy texture that is not everyone's cup of tea. Nameko are not found fresh, but bottled or tinned. Light brown and with small round caps, they are covered in a clear, gelatinous and slippery substance. Traditionally, nameko are found at breakfast, floating in miso soup or served with grated daikon radish and vinegared soy sauce as a side dish.

- **Shiitake** Available fresh or dried, these mushrooms are a staple ingredient for the Japanese pantry with their deep umami flavour. Dried shiitake have a strong woody taste and substantial meaty texture. Once rehydrated in water they are ready to add to dishes, soaking up flavourful broths and sauces. They also hold their shape during slow-cooking, making them the perfect addition to a stew. Fresh shiitake have a delicate and slippery texture when cooked so the dried version is more suited to long, slow cooking. High in vitamins B and C, low in calories yet rich in flavour, shiitake are one of Japan's miracle foods, believed to prevent cancer and lead to a long life. Japanese dried shiitake mushrooms are shockingly expensive, but you can source dried shiitake from Chinese/Asian supermarkets that are much cheaper and a good substitute.

- **Shimeji** These little button-like mushrooms are increasingly found in the West, particularly *buna shimeji*. *Buna shimeji* grow in bunches of tight clusters – each mushroom joined at the bottom, with white stems topped with brown caps that are similar in size to enoki. They have little flavour or aroma of their own but have a substantially rich and meaty texture and are enjoyed in soups, stir-fries or cooked in rice. These mushrooms last a fairly long time in the fridge (about 10 days), so they are good to keep on hand.

YAM CAKE AND POTATO STEW

This is my vegetarian take on *niku-jaga*, which is a very traditional beef and potato stew. Without the beef, the ginger is less muted and comes into its own.

SERVES 4

Peel and cut the potatoes into large bite-sized pieces. Soak in a bowl of cold water for 5 minutes.

Prepare the yam cakes by placing in a bowl. Pour over just-boiled water to cover and soak for 1 minute. Rinse with cold water and drain. Cut each cake along the shortest side of the rectangular shape into 7mm thick slices, so you will have 7.5cm x 2cm x 7mm *konnyaku* slices. Make a 5cm score in the middle and then push one side through into the score, so it looks like a plait. Repeat this for the remaining slices.

Heat the oil in a large saucepan over a medium heat and add the onions. Sauté for 2 minutes, then add the potatoes and carrots and stir-fry for 1 minute.

In a separate frying pan, heat the sesame oil and fry the yam cake slices for 2 minutes on each side over a medium heat. Remove and transfer to the pan with the potatoes. Pour over the dashi stock, the soy sauce, mirin, sake, sugar and dried shiitake mushrooms. Bring to the boil over a high heat, turn the heat down to medium-low and simmer for 30–40 minutes, or until the potatoes and carrots are soft but not breaking up. Keep an eye on the liquid and add more stock if it looks dry. Season to taste with salt.

Add the mangetout to the pan and cook for a further 1 minute. Divide into individual bowls, making sure each ingredient is equally portioned, and then top with the ginger and serve immediately.

800g potatoes
400g yam cake (*konnyaku*) (2 cakes)
2 tablespoons sunflower or vegetable oil
2 onions, cut into thin wedges
4 carrots, cut into 2cm cubes
1 tablespoon sesame oil
1.5 litres vegetarian dashi stock (see page 166), or 2 teaspoons kombu dashi powder mixed with 1.5 litres hot water
80ml soy sauce
3 tablespoons mirin
2 tablespoons sake
2 tablespoons sugar
8 dried shiitake mushrooms
120g mangetout or sugar snap peas
40g ginger, cut into fine matchsticks, to serve
sea salt

MOCHI AND GREENS
WITH WALNUT MISO PESTO

This is one of my favourite dishes in the book. It is so rich and creamy. The unique combination of ingredients and flavours are not at all traditional, but of my own devising. I think they work beautifully together.

SERVES 4

200g asparagus
100g *shiratamako*
   (sweet rice flour)
2 tablespoons olive oil
200g spinach
shichimi pepper, to serve
sea salt

**FOR THE WALNUT AND
   WHITE MISO PESTO**
100g walnuts
60g white miso
3 tablespoons soy sauce
3 tablespoons mirin
2 teaspoons rice vinegar
1–2 teaspoons sugar

Trim the tough part of the asparagus stalks off and discard. Cut the asparagus into 5cm pieces, on the diagonal. Set aside.

Make the walnut and miso pesto. Toast the walnuts in a dry frying pan over a low heat, shaking the pan occasionally, until a shade darker. Put into a small food processor (or use a mortar and pestle) with the remaining pesto ingredients and blitz to combine. Be careful not to over-blitz as you want a rough paste with some texture.

To make the mochi, put the flour into a large bowl. Slowly add 180–200ml of warm water, mixing until combined. Knead to form a soft, smooth dough for about 3 minutes. Form the dough into balls about the size of golf balls. Next, use a thumb to press the centre of each ball gently to make an indentation.

Bring a large saucepan of water to the boil and then add a pinch of salt. Drop the balls into the boiling water and cook for about 2 minutes, or until the balls are floating on the surface of water. Scoop them out using a slotted spoon and then dip them in a bowl of cold water straight away. Drain.

Heat a large frying pan with olive oil and add the asparagus and a pinch of salt. Cook over a medium heat for about 3–4 minutes, tossing the spears in the pan, or until just cooked but still crunchy. Turn up the heat and add the spinach and cook for about 1 minute, by tossing and mixing until the spinach is just cooked, adding a little hot water if necessary.

Add the vegetables and pesto to a large bowl and toss, making sure the pesto evenly coats the vegetables. Add the mochi balls to the bowl and gently toss. Serve immediately with shichimi pepper on the side.

OKRA AND TOFU CURRY

This is my kind of fusion Japanese curry. I just love the pairing of okra and paneer in Indian cuisine so I replaced the paneer with tofu. And that's how this dish was born. All flavours work with Japanese curry roux.

SERVES 4

In a large saucepan, heat the oil and sauté the leek and onion over a medium heat for about 3 minutes. Add the ginger and pepper and sauté for a further 2 minutes. Pour in 800ml of water, then bring to the boil. Once it comes to the boil, add the curry roux and stir to break it up in the pan. Turn the heat down to medium-low and mix to ensure there are no lumps of roux.

Add the coconut milk, tofu cubes and arame seaweed to the pan and bring back to the boil. Turn the heat down to low and simmer for 7–8 minutes.

While the curry sauce is being cooked, heat the oil for deep-frying in a wok or medium-sized saucepan to 170°C.

Dust the okra in the flour, then quickly deep-fry for about 1 minute, making sure to keep the okra moving around in the oil. Remove with a slotted spoon and drain on kitchen paper. Transfer immediately to the curry sauce and turn off the heat. Doing so will keep the bright green colour and crunchiness of the okra.

Toast or grill your bread of choice, if using. Divide the curry mixture into individual bowls. Top with chopped boiled eggs and deep-fried shallots. Serve with pita breads or rice on the side.

2 tablespoons sunflower or
   vegetable oil, plus an extra
   500ml for deep-frying
½ leek, finely chopped
1 onion, finely chopped
2 teaspoons grated ginger
1 yellow pepper, cored
   and diced
200g Japanese curry roux
400ml coconut milk
250g firm tofu, cut into
   1.5cm cubes
15g dried arame seaweed
250g okra, cut into
   bite-sized pieces
2 tablespoons plain flour

TO SERVE
4–6 brown pita breads or 600g
   freshly cooked short-grain rice
   (see page 168)
2 hard-boiled eggs, peeled
   and chopped
deep-fried shallots

TOFU KATSU CURRY

The *katsu* style of a crumbed cutlet deep-fried is a great way of condensing the flavour of your chosen protein. With this dish, you can enjoy the sweetness and texture of tofu with curry sauce. Use firm tofu. Although it is fried it remains very light.

SERVES 4

2 tablespoons sunflower or
   vegetable oil
2 large onions, finely chopped
2 garlic cloves, finely chopped
1 tablespoon peeled and
   grated ginger
2 carrots, peeled and
   finely chopped
2 courgettes, finely chopped
200g chestnut mushrooms,
   roughly chopped
1 tablespoon curry powder
4 tablespoons sake
200g Japanese curry roux
1 apple, grated
600g freshly cooked short-grain
   rice (see page 168)
pickled fennel and courgette
   (see page 162) or daikon with
   plum vinegar (see page 159),
   to serve, optional

FOR THE TOFU KATSU
600g firm tofu
4 tablespoons plain flour
2 eggs
100g panko breadcrumbs
1 litre sunflower or vegetable oil,
   for deep-frying
sea salt and ground white pepper

To prepare the tofu, wrap in kitchen paper and press between 2 chopping boards with a weight (such as a tin of beans) on the top. Arrange in the sink on a slight angle, so that excess water can drain away. Leave for 1–2 hours.

Heat 2 tablespoons of oil in a large saucepan over a medium-high heat and sauté the onions, garlic, grated ginger and carrots for 7–8 minutes. Add the courgettes and mushrooms and stir-fry for 1 minute. Stir in the curry powder, and keep the ingredients moving for about 3 minutes. Pour in the sake and continue to cook for about 1 minute to allow the alcohol to evaporate.

Pour 720ml of water into the pan and bring to the boil over a high heat. Reduce the heat to medium-low, then add the curry roux, breaking it up with a spoon. Stir well until all the roux has dissolved. Add the grated apple and simmer for 15–20 minutes, stirring from time to time.

Meanwhile, prepare the tofu katsu. Unwrap the tofu and cut into 4 equal portions. Put the flour in a shallow bowl and season with salt and white pepper. Beat the eggs lightly in a bowl and put the panko crumbs on a plate. Dust each tofu cube with the seasoned flour, dip into the eggs, then coat in panko crumbs, making sure all the surfaces are covered completely in the crumbs.

Heat the oil in a large pan or deep-fryer to 170°C and then slide the tofu into the hot oil. Deep-fry for 2–3 minutes, until golden in colour. Use a slotted spoon to remove and drain on layers of kitchen paper.

Serve the rice in large serving bowls and pour in some of the curry sauce. Arrange the tofu katsu on top. Have the pickled vegetables in a small bowl to serve with the curry.

EDAMAME AND TOFU TERIYAKI BURGER

Edamame and tofu are both super healthy and high in protein. This burger gives you your fill of energy and is low in calories. And it's still a burger! The burgers can be served with plain rice instead of burger buns.

SERVES 4

To prepare the tofu, wrap in kitchen paper and press between 2 chopping boards with a weight (such as a tin of beans) on the top. Arrange in the sink on a slight angle, so that excess water can drain away. Leave for 1–2 hours.

Bring a pan of water to the boil with a pinch of salt and add the edamame. Cook for 3–4 minutes. Once the edamame is cooked, drain and rinse under cold water. Place in a colander to drain completely.

Heat 2 tablespoons of the oil in a frying pan and sauté the leek with a pinch of salt for 4–5 minutes, then add the soy sauce and mirin and cook gently for a further 3–4 minutes, or until most of the liquid evaporates.

Put the edamame in a food processor and blitz until slightly smooth but still with a little bit of texture. Combine with the leek and grated ginger in a large bowl.

Add the tofu to the bowl, crumbling it in your hands, and stir through the edamame mixture. Add the wakame flakes, egg and panko breadcrumbs and mix well. If the mixture is too soft, add more panko crumbs. If it is too dry and hard, add a little bit of soy sauce or mirin.

Put the flour on a plate and season with salt and pepper.

Divide the mixture into small portions of 8 or large portions of 4. Shape into balls and flatten slightly to make burgers. Dust the burgers with seasoned flour, making sure they are well coated.

Heat the remaining 2 tablespoons of oil in a large frying pan and fry the burgers, in batches, for 4–5 minutes on each side.

While the burgers are cooking, make the wasabi mayonnaise by mixing the mayonnaise with the wasabi in a small bowl. Adjust the amount of wasabi as you like. Serve the burgers encased in the buns with lettuce, wasabi mayo and teriyaki sauce.

200g firm tofu
400g podded frozen
    edamame beans
4 tablespoons sunflower
    or vegetable oil
2 small leeks, finely chopped
4 tablespoons soy sauce
4 tablespoons mirin
1 tablespoon freshly
    grated ginger
8g dried wakame seaweed
    flakes, crushed
1 egg, lightly beaten
2 tablespoons panko
    breadcrumbs or dried
    breadcrumbs
2 tablespoons plain flour
sea salt and freshly ground
    white pepper

FOR THE WASABI MAYO (OR USE SHOP-BOUGHT)
4–5 tablespoons Japanese
    mayonnaise (see page 167)
    or shop-bought mayonnaise
1½ teaspoons grated fresh
    wasabi or wasabi paste

TO SERVE
4 brioche burger buns
4 large leaves iceberg lettuce
4 tablespoons teriyaki sauce
    (see page 167)

POPULAR VEGETABLES IN JAPANESE COOKING

The vegetables noted here are used on a daily basis in Japan, but are to be found in most Western countries too. Although we use spinach, spring onion and sweet potato here in the UK, the Japanese versions are quite different in size and texture, and the flavours tend to be much denser and deeper.

- **Bamboo shoot (*takenoko*)** This is one of the classic vegetables of East Asia. The uniqueness of the crisp texture makes this mountain vegetable special, although it contains very few nutrients.

- **Chinese cabbage (*hakusai*)** In recent years, Chinese cabbage has become one of the most popular leafy vegetables in Japanese cooking due to its versatility. Chinese cabbage is often used for stews and lends itself well to being lightly pickled.

- **Daikon radish** A long and white radish, also known as mooli. It is the most versatile of vegetables and can be shredded to garnish sashimi or as a condiment to sashimi. Daikon also works well in simmered dishes and lends itself to pickling.

- **Ginger (*tuchi shoga*)** This is the most commonly used spice in Japan. The reason is twofold. It is considered to be very healthy, and it has a fantastic flavour. As ginger is known to help digestion, it's often served with deep-fried dishes to help break down the fat. It is used both raw, either freshly grated or thinly sliced and cooked, and also pickled to accompany sushi.

- **Japanese lime (*yuzu*)** *Yuzu* is regarded as a precious citrus fruit for Japanese cooking, and it reaches a high price due to its seasonality. The fruit can be used to flavour sorbets and desserts, or as a sweet coulis-type dressing. Fresh *yuzu* is difficult to get hold of outside of Japan, but concentrated yuzu juice is available in bottles.

- **Japanese pumpkin (*kabocha*)** A deep green, ragged-skinned pumpkin that is much smaller than the Western pumpkin. *Kabocha* pumpkins have very dense and deep orange flesh, and are a good source of nutrients. They are traditionally used in simmered dishes or tempura. In recent years, they have also been popular in soups or desserts.

- **Lotus root (*renkon*)** When sliced, lotus roots tend to look like flowers with holes forming each 'petal'. The flavour is not distinct but the texture is crunchy, and the appearance makes any dish look impressive.

- **Spinach (*horensou*)** Japanese spinach is much firmer than the typical variety found in the West, with stems that become reddish-coloured close to the roots.

- **Spring onion (*negi*)** There are two types of spring onion in Japan: one is very long and thick while the other is thinner but not as small and fine as those available in the West. Spring onions are used in many dishes either as a garnish or as an ingredient in their own right, fried or simmered. They are the equivalent to onion for Western cooking.

- **Sweet potato (*satsuma imo*)** *Satsuma* is the old name for the southern region of Japan and *imo* means potato. Japanese sweet potato is long with burgundy skin and pale yellow flesh, and its texture is less stringy than pumpkin and more glutinous than potato.

- **Tokyo turnip (*kabu*)** Smaller than the Western turnip, this cooks quickly and has appeared in upmarket restaurants in recent years. It has a slightly bitter flavour and the leaves have a strong flavour.

PURPLE POTATO CROQUETTES

Potato croquettes may have originated in France but they quickly spread worldwide. In Japan they are well-favoured and called *korokke*. Typically, this delicious fried street food is made of panko-crumbed mashed potatoes with onion and mince. My vegetarian version is just as flavoursome and uses sweet potato for an interesting twist.

SERVES 4

2 tablespoons sunflower or
    vegetable oil, plus 1 litre,
    for deep-frying
500g purple sweet potato,
    peeled and cut into 2cm chunks
1 carrot, peeled and sliced
    into wide ribbons using a
    mandoline or vegetable peeler
1 courgette, sliced into wide
    ribbons using a mandoline or
    vegetable peeler
60ml milk
125g plain flour
2 eggs
100g panko breadcrumbs
sea salt and ground white pepper
iceberg lettuce, to serve

FOR THE GINGER, SESAME
AND PONZU SAUCE
6 tablespoons soy sauce
2 tablespoons rice vinegar
2 tablespoons sugar
2 tablespoons grated ginger
3 tablespoons toasted and
    ground sesame seeds

FOR THE YUZU MAYO
1 egg yolk
4 tablespoons yuzu juice
6 tablespoons Japanese
    mayonnaise (see page 167),
    or shop-bought
½ teaspoon sugar

Preheat the oven to 240°C/220°C fan/gas mark 9.

Coat clean hands with some oil and then rub each potato chunk to coat with the oil. Place in a roasting tray and sprinkle with a little salt. Cover lightly with foil and bake for about 20 minutes or until the potatoes are just cooked.

Bring plenty of water to the boil in a large pan and add a pinch of salt and the carrot and courgette. Boil for 1 minute, then remove from the heat and drain. Rinse under cold water, then drain and pat dry with kitchen paper. Cut those ribbons to about 5cm lengths.

Remove the potatoes from the oven and transfer to a bowl. Add the milk and then mash with a potato masher until there are no lumps.

Combine the flour and a pinch each of salt and white pepper on a plate. Whisk the eggs in a bowl, and put the panko breadcrumbs on a plate.

Choose a ring or cup that is about 5cm in diameter – this will be used as the mould. Divide the mashed potatoes into 12 portions. Put a third of the mashed potato at the bottom of each mould, followed by the carrots and courgettes, then repeat the layering and finish with the mashed potato. Take off the mould, holding it all together firmly, and press using both hands to form a compact patty. Repeat for the remaining mashed potato and vegetables, then dust each patty with flour well. Next, dip into the eggs and then into the panko crumbs, making sure the surface of the patty is well coated.

Heat the oil in a wok or large frying pan to 160°C. Carefully add the patties, in batches, to the hot oil and deep-fry for 3 minutes (depending on the size of the patty), turning them over a few times. Once golden brown, remove onto kitchen paper or a wire rack to drain the excess oil.

To make the ginger, sesame and ponzu sauce, simply combine all the ingredients in a bowl.

To make the yuzu mayonnaise, whisk the egg yolk and yuzu juice together in a bowl. Add the mayonnaise and sugar and mix well until the sugar has dissolved.

Serve the croquettes with crispy shredded iceberg lettuce and sauces on the side.

SPINACH AND MUSHROOM RICE GRATIN
WITH WHITE MISO SAUCE

It's my French-Japanese fusion dish. Japanese love both French food and the combination of rice and miso. In this dish you can have it all. It can easily be cooked in individual baking dishes, just reduce the cooking time slightly.

SERVES 4

Trim the base of the shimeji mushrooms and separate into clumps.

Heat a large frying pan with the oil and stir-fry the mushrooms with a little salt and pepper, over a medium-high heat, for about 2 minutes. Once they are just cooked, remove and set aside on kitchen paper.

Preheat the oven to 180°C/160°C fan/gas mark 4.

Bring a pan of water to the boil with a pinch of salt. Add the spinach and blanch for 30 seconds, drain and rinse under cold water until the leaves are cold. Drain and squeeze the excess water out. Roughly chop and combine with the cooked shimeji mushrooms in a bowl.

Put the eggs in a saucepan and cover with water. Set over a medium-high heat and once you start to see small bubbles at the edge of the pan, set a timer for 4 minutes. Drain and place the eggs in a bowl of cold water to come to room temperature. Peel once cooled and cut each egg into quarters.

To make the miso sauce, melt the butter in a saucepan over a low heat and add the flour. Cook out the flour for 1 minute, stirring to make it into a thick, smooth paste. Pour in the milk, little by little, whisking all the time to ensure the mixture doesn't become lumpy. Keep stirring, then add in the miso and mustard. Cook for 3 minutes, until well combined and thickened. Season with salt and pepper to taste.

In a small bowl, combine the grated cheese with the panko breadcrumbs and chopped chives.

Brush a large casserole dish with oil. Add the spinach and mushroom mixture and spread out evenly over the base of the dish. Scatter over the rice and spread out, then place the quartered boiled eggs on top of the rice. Pour over the white miso sauce, making sure to completely cover the surface. Sprinkle with the breadcrumb and cheese mixture and bake for about 30 minutes, or until the edges start to bubble and the top becomes a light golden colour.

Serve sprinkled with the extra chopped chives.

300g shimeji mushrooms
2 tablespoons olive oil
400g spinach
4 large eggs
150g choice of hard cheese (parmesan, pecorino, cheddar), grated
2 tablespoons panko breadcrumbs
2 tablespoons finely chopped chives, plus extra to serve
sunflower or vegetable oil
400g freshly cooked short-grain rice (see page 168), cold
sea salt and ground white pepper

FOR THE WHITE MISO SAUCE
80g butter
80g plain flour
1 litre soy milk, at room temperature
80g white miso
1 teaspoon Dijon mustard

MISO-CURED TOFU

This could be considered the 'dish of the book'. Using the red miso cure creates a salty and sweet flavour profile, which penetrates deep into the silken tofu. This in turn becomes denser and creamier. It's a wonderful texture and a sensational dish.

The directions below partner the cured tofu with grilled bread and pickled vegetables. It can also be eaten simply with crusty bread, or accompanied by kombu broth or a crunchy salad. The cured tofu itself will keep, covered, for two to three days in the fridge.

SERVES 4

4 tablespoons mirin
4 tablespoons sake
150g red miso
150g koji miso
2 x 300g blocks silken tofu

TO SERVE
1 ciabatta loaf or baguette
50–60ml olive oil
1 teaspoon sea salt
1 tablespoon grated fresh
   wasabi or wasabi paste
handful of pea shoots
daikon with plum vinegar
   (see page 159), to serve
red miso-pickled carrot and
   daikon (see page 164),
   to serve

Heat the mirin and sake in a small saucepan over a high heat and bring to the boil. Allow the alcohol to boil away and evaporate slightly, for about 30 seconds. Stir in both misos and mix well.

Cut each 300g tofu block in half so you have 4 portions. Bring a large saucepan of water to the boil and add the tofu. Simmer over a medium heat for about 3 minutes. Remove from the heat and drain. Place on a few layers of kitchen paper and allow to drain and cool to room temperature. Change the kitchen paper once during this time.

Spread a third of the miso mixture across the bottom a large, wide and shallow plastic container. Place the cooled tofu squares on top and then tightly wrap with a thin muslin cloth. Spread the remaining miso mixture over the top of the muslin, making sure you cover the tops and sides of the tofu portions. Put the lid on the container and store at cool room temperature for 3–4 days (by the window is ideal).

To serve, slice the bread of your choice and drizzle with olive oil. Grill the slices on both sides, until golden, and sprinkle with the salt.

Carefully remove the cured tofu from the muslin and scrape off the miso mixture. Slice the tofu into large cubes and then transfer to individual plates or shallow bowls. Garnish with the wasabi and some pea shoots and serve with the grilled bread and the pickles.

TIP
Silken tofu is fragile, and will be even more so after marinating for 3 days. Using a muslin cloth makes it easier to remove the marinade from the tofu without it breaking. The miso will penetrate through the muslin, so you won't lose any flavour.

TOFU

Tofu is an important ingredient in savoury Japanese dishes, with a delicate flavour and excellent nutritional value. It is also a great source of protein, amino acids, iron, calcium and other essential nutrients, while being naturally gluten free and low in fat and calories.

The ancient city of Kyoto is renowned for its tofu, which has been perfected over time by Buddhist monks. Tofu artisans use centuries-old techniques to create perfect blocks of fresh, silky and surprisingly tasty tofu that is very different from the mass-produced variety usually found in supermarkets. Freshly made tofu is creamy and subtly sweet and should be sought out if at all possible.

Tofu is made with soy beans and a coagulant called *nigari*, which can be bought all over Japan or at Asian supermarkets worldwide. During the process of making tofu, soy beans are soaked and crushed, puréed, heated up and strained to extract the soy milk. *Nigari* is mixed with the fresh soy milk and the mix is transferred into moulds.

TOFU VARIETIES

There are different varieties of tofu, and different levels of firmness:
  Oboro – runny (custard-like consistency)
  Kinugoshi – silken
  Momen – cotton (firm)

One of the best ways to enjoy silken tofu is as it is, with grated ginger, finely chopped spring onions and soy sauce on top. Another popular dish from Kyoto is *yudofu*, simply fondu tofu in a water bath and ginger-soy dipping sauce.

Around Japan you can find artisan tofu makers who devote their expertise to perfecting the art of making this ingredient. Tofu is revered in Japan, and Kyoto in particular is famous for the delicacy of its tofu, but in the West this ingredient is often neglected or considered vegetarian-only food. I believe tofu has a subtle and stunning flavour by itself, but it also has the ability to adapt and can easily absorb other flavours to make an altogether delicious dish. Indeed, there is a type of traditional, refined Japanese cuisine known as *tofu kaiseki* that uses tofu in every dish, and in all its different forms, from a hot pot to a soup or even a French-inspired gratin (see page 147). *Tofu kaiseki* is a light meal that is definitely something to try if you visit Kyoto.

When buying, always opt for the best tofu you can source. The good news is that it's now much easier to obtain reasonably good-quality tofu outside of Japan. I hope the recipes in this book will give you an appreciation of this unique and delicious ingredient.

TOFU VENDOR'S TRUMPET

Before large supermarkets made an appearance, many traditional ingredients were sold by individual sellers. Growing up in Japan, I remember hearing a single trumpet early each morning: the tofu man's trumpet! My mother would go out with a bowl to buy a tofu square from him each morning. This is one of many culinary memories of my mother.

TOFU STEAKS
WITH MISO SPINACH AND MUSHROOMS

This tasty and super healthy tofu dish is a great main as it is very filling and has it all. You can serve it with rice or noodles, or as is.

SERVES 4

To prepare the tofu, wrap in kitchen paper and press between 2 chopping boards with a weight (such as a tin of beans) on the top. Arrange in the sink on a slight angle, so that excess water can drain away. Leave for 1–2 hours.

Bring a pan of water to the boil with a pinch of salt and blanch the spinach leaves for 10 seconds. Drain and rinse under cold water until the spinach becomes cold. Drain again and squeeze any excess water out, then roughly chop.

Remove the tofu from the boards and pat dry with kitchen paper. Cut into 8–12 slices and pat each slice with more kitchen paper. Season the cornflour with salt and white pepper and then dust the tofu slices with this seasoned flour, making sure all the tofu surfaces are covered.

Heat 60ml of the oil in a frying pan over a medium heat and fry the tofu for about 3 minutes each side, or until crisp and light golden in colour.

Next, combine the mirin, soy sauce and miso with 4 tablespoons of water in a small bowl until there are no lumps.

Heat the butter or sesame oil and remaining 30ml of sunflower or vegetable oil in a wok or large frying pan over a medium heat. Add the ginger, spring onions, mushrooms and yellow pepper and stir-fry for 2 minutes and then add the drained spinach. Immediately pour in the miso mixture, and cook for a further 1 minute or until 80 per cent of the liquid has evaporated.

Arrange the tofu on a serving plate and top with the miso spinach and mushrooms. Make sure not to cover the entire tofu otherwise it will turn soggy. Sprinkle toasted sesame seeds on top.

600g firm tofu
200g baby spinach leaves
3 tablespoons cornflour
90ml sunflower or vegetable oil
4 tablespoons mirin
2 tablespoons soy sauce
60g white miso
20g butter or 1 tablespoon sesame oil
100g ginger, peeled and finely grated
4 spring onions, finely chopped
160g shiitake mushrooms, stalks removed and caps thinly sliced
1 yellow pepper, cored and thinly sliced
1 tablespoon toasted sesame seeds
sea salt and ground white pepper

YUZU MISO-GLAZED AUBERGINE
WITH LOTUS ROOT CRISPS

This dish is a twist on the traditional miso-glazed aubergines (*nasu dengaku*) using the emblematic Japanese citrus, *yuzu*. The fruit's sweet and tangy flavour goes very well with the richness of the miso, and the lotus root crisps add a nice crunch and texture contrast.

SERVES 4

2 aubergines
4 tablespoons sunflower or
    vegetable oil, plus an extra
    500ml for deep-frying
300g lotus root
zest of 1 yuzu or lime
sea salt

FOR THE YUZU MISO
200g white miso
2 tablespoons sugar
2 tablespoons mirin
½ teaspoon kombu
    dashi powder
5 tablespoons yuzu juice
1 egg yolk

Preheat the oven to 230°C/210°C fan/gas mark 8.

Cut the aubergines in half horizontally and arrange on a roasting tray. Brush 2 tablespoons of the oil on the cut side of the aubergines and cover the tray with foil. Bake for about 10 minutes, then remove the foil and brush the remaining oil over the top and return to the oven for a further 10 minutes, or until the aubergines are just cooked. To check they are done, poke the thickest part of the flesh with a skewer – it should slide through smoothly. If you feel resistance, then it needs more cooking.

Meanwhile, mix the miso, sugar, mirin and dashi powder with 100ml of water in a small saucepan over very low heat. Cook for 3–4 minutes, stir in the yuzu juice and continue to simmer for 1 more minute. Add the egg yolk and cook, over a low heat and stirring all the time, for about 2 minutes or until the miso mixture becomes quite thick. Leave it to cool.

Have ready a bowl of cold water with about 1 teaspoon of salt stirred in. Peel and thinly slice the lotus root and, as you go, put the slices in the bowl of salted water. Rinse under cold water, drain and pat dry with kitchen paper. Heat the 500ml of oil in a large pan until it comes up to 150°C. Add the lotus root and deep-fry for 2 minutes, until light golden in colour. Remove with a slotted spoon and drain on kitchen paper. The lotus root crisps can be made in advance – they will keep in an airtight container for up to 1 week.

Pre-heat the grill to medium-high.

Arrange the aubergine on a baking tray. Spoon the yuzu miso paste on top of the aubergines and spread over thickly to cover the entire surface. Place under the grill for a couple of minutes, until the mixture bubbles up.

Grate the yuzu or lime zest over the aubergines and serve with the lotus root crisps on the side.

PICKLES
AND
BASICS

CABBAGE AND CUCUMBER PICKLE
WITH GINGER

Asazuke is a quick method for pickling vegetables, commonly reserved for daikon radish, cucumbers or aubergines. This combination of cabbage, cucumber and ginger is a very popular one. You can enjoy the pickles in their own right, as part of a salad.

SERVES 4

10g dried kombu
½ head of Chinese cabbage
1 large cucumber, cut into 5cm
    length batons
1 tablespoon sea salt
1 teaspoon kombu dashi powder
2 teaspoons sugar
1 tablespoon mirin
3 tablespoons rice vinegar
100g ginger, peeled and sliced
    then cut into needle-like sticks
1 red chilli, sliced (optional)

Put the kombu in a bowl with 220ml of water and leave to soak for 20 minutes.

Cut the Chinese cabbage into 2cm-wide chunks. Separate the white part of the cabbage from the green leafy part. Rub and massage the white part of cabbage and the cucumber with the salt and toss in a large bowl for about 2 minutes. Add the green leafy parts of the cabbage and then gently massage for another 30 seconds. The salt will draw out a lot of water from the vegetables. Leave to sit for 5 minutes in a colander.

Take the kombu out of the water, making sure to reserve the soaking water, and slice it very finely.

In a large bowl, add the dashi powder, sugar, mirin and vinegar with the reserved kombu soaking water. Mix well and then add the vegetables. Toss and mix well. Transfer to an airtight jar and keep in the fridge for at least for 2–3 hours. Best consumed within 2 days.

DAIKON
WITH PLUM VINEGAR

Simply beautiful. This lightly pink-coloured and paper-thin daikon is the most delicate pickle. It has a subtle beauty and is great as a condiment for sushi.

SERVES 8

To make the plum vinegar, prepare the plums by removing the stones. Cut the flesh into large chunks. Pour the vinegar into a large jar and add the sugar and salt. Shake the jar well to dissolve the sugar and salt completely. Add the plum chunks and leave to pickle for at least 24 hours at room temperature. If you want stronger colour, you can leave it for longer.

Peel and slice the daikon radish against the fibre using a mandoline – you're aiming for very thin slices, almost see-through.

Place the sliced daikon in a large container, sprinkle with the salt and then pour the plum vinegar with a few plum chunks into the container until the daikon is completely submerged in vinegar. Add the kombu pieces.

Leave to pickle in the fridge for at least 24 hours. Check the pickle a couple of times, moving the daikon around to make sure it is submerged in the pickling liquid. Keeps for 3–4 days in the fridge.

800g daikon radish
1 tablespoon salt
5g dried kombu, cut into pieces

FOR THE PLUM VINEGAR
4 red plums
600ml rice vinegar
3 tablespoons sugar
1 teaspoon sea salt

Clockwise from left: Daikon (see page 159); Cabbage and Cucumber Pickle (see page 158); Red Miso-Pickled Carrot (see page164); Pickled Yellow Pepper (see page 166); Yuzu-Pickled Celery (see page 165)

PICKLED FENNEL AND COURGETTE

Both fennel and courgette are considered Western vegetables in Japan. Both, though, pickle so well in the Japanese style. They make a perfect side dish for Tofu Karaage Rice Bowl (see page 88) and Tofu Katsu Curry (see page 138), and similar mains.

SERVES 8

1 large fennel bulb, sliced very thinly using a mandoline or vegetable peeler
1 courgette, sliced very thinly using a mandoline or vegetable peeler
2 teaspoons sea salt
zest of ½ lemon, thinly sliced (optional)
1 chilli, thinly sliced (optional)

FOR THE PICKLING LIQUID
1 teaspoon kombu dashi powder
220ml rice vinegar
2 tablespoons sugar
2 tablespoons lemon juice

Place the fennel and courgette slices in a large bowl, and add the salt. Using clean hands, rub and massage the salt gently into the vegetables for 1–2 minutes until the vegetables start to release water. Rinse with water.

To make the pickling liquid, mix the dashi powder with 1 tablespoon of water in a large bowl. Pour in the vinegar, then add the sugar and lemon juice. Mix well, making sure the dashi powder and sugar have dissolved completely.

Add the fennel and courgettes to the bowl with the pickling liquid and toss well. Add the lemon zest and chilli at this point if you wish. Leave to pickle for at least for 30 minutes.

Once made, this will keep for up to 3 days.

TIP
This is also delicious made with cucumber in place of the courgette.

PICKLED TURNIP
WITH CHILLI AND WAKAME

Turnip is my favourite pickled vegetable, and I have created a rather magical version using wakame seaweed. The natural sweetness from wakame and chilli provides a wonderful flavouring to the turnip.

SERVES 8

Rinse the turnips well. Trim away the top hard parts and the bottom pointy bits. Cut each turnip into 8–12 segments, depending on the size of the turnip.

Place in a bowl with the salt. Use clean hands to rub and massage the salt into the turnip for about 2 minutes. Rinse well under cold water and drain.

To make the pickling liquid, pour 260ml of water into a large bowl and stir in the dashi powder, vinegar, sugar and salt. Mix well to ensure the salt and sugar have dissolved. Add the turnip, dried wakame flakes and chillies to an airtight jar.

Allow to pickle for at least 1 day. Once made, this will keep for up to 3 days.

4 turnips
1 tablespoon sea salt
2 tablespoons dried
    wakame flakes
4 bird's eye chillies

FOR THE PICKLING LIQUID
2 teaspoons kombu
    dashi powder
3 tablespoons rice vinegar
1 tablespoon sugar
1 teaspoon sea salt

RED MISO-PICKLED CARROT
AND DAIKON

One word describes this pickle: addictive. It takes two days for the flavours to develop but I guarantee it is worth the wait. The umami from the addition of miso penetrates the vegetables, giving them the deepest flavour.

**MAKES ENOUGH TO FILL A
750ML JAR**

500g daikon radish
2 carrots
2 tablespoons sea salt
100g red miso
1 teaspoon kombu dashi powder
6 tablespoons mirin
2 tablespoons rice vinegar
1 teaspoon sugar
½ onion, thinly sliced

Peel the daikon and then cut in half. Cut each half into quarters, lengthways, to make 8 pieces. Aim for batons about 10cm x 2cm. Cut the carrots into slightly thinner chunks than the daikon. Place the daikon and carrots into 2 separate bowls.

Sprinkle 1 tablespoon of the salt over the carrots and the remaining tablespoon over the daikon. Use clean hands to massage the salt into the vegetables, for about 1 minute each. The salt will draw out a lot of water from the vegetables. Rinse under cold water, then drain and pat dry with kitchen paper.

In a bowl, combine the miso, dashi powder, mirin, vinegar, sugar and onion. Stir well to make sure the sugar has dissolved.

Put the miso mixture into a plastic container with a lid. Add the daikon and carrot chunks to the container and spread the miso mixture over the top, making sure to cover all of the daikon with the mixture. Put the lid on and refrigerate for 2–3 days. Each day, take the container out of the fridge and give the vegetables a gentle stir.

When the pickle is ready, scrape away the miso mixture and serve. This will keep in the fridge for up to 5 days.

YUZU-PICKLED CELERY
AND OYSTER MUSHROOMS

You don't see many pickled mushrooms around, and celery is not the most popular vegetable in Japan. So this led to my take on fusion pickles and I love it! The sweet and citrussy yuzu flavour is in perfect harmony.

SERVES 4

Heat the vinegar, sugar and salt in a small saucepan over a low heat and stir to melt the sugar. Simmer for 6–7 minutes to allow it to reduce a little – it should be slightly syrupy in consistency. Leave to cool.

Wash the celery stalks and trim off the top and bottom ends, removing the stringy bits from the celery.

Soak the hijiki in 250ml of water for 15–20 minutes.

Clean the mushrooms by rubbing them with damp kitchen paper and then cut off the hard part of the stalk. Slice the mushrooms into thin pieces and sprinkle with 1 teaspoon of salt. Use clean hands to gently massage the salt into the mushrooms, then rinse off under cold water. Drain and squeeze any excess water out.

Place the pickling liquid in a large bowl, drain the seaweed and add to the bowl along with the celery and mushrooms. Pour in the yuzu and toss gently. Take a slightly smaller bowl, fill it with water or weights such as canned tomatoes, and place on top of the vegetables in the bowl (this will press out excess moisture). Leave for at least 30 minutes, mix and then leave for a further 15 minutes until the celery has softened considerably.

Leave to sit at room temperature for 3 hours, then it's ready to eat. Keeps refrigerated for up to 2 days.

8 inner tender celery stalks
20g dried hijiki seaweed
200g oyster mushrooms
1 teaspoon sea salt
60ml yuzu juice

FOR THE PICKLING LIQUID
4 tablespoons rice vinegar
4 tablespoons sugar
1 teaspoon sea salt

PICKLED YELLOW PEPPER
AND ARAME SEAWEED

This is the boldest pickle I've ever created. Peppers are never pickled in Japan, but I wanted something striking in appearance and appealing in flavour to the Western palette. And here it is.

**MAKES ENOUGH TO FILL
A 750ML JAR**

20g dried arame seaweed
2 yellow peppers
2 large red chillies
1 teaspoon kombu dashi powder
1 teaspoon sea salt
1 tablespoon sugar
2½ tablespoons rice vinegar

Soak the dried arame seaweed in a bowl of water for about 5 minutes. Drain.

Remove the stem and core from the peppers and slice into short (about 1cm) sticks. Slice the chillies into thin rings.

In a large bowl, pour in 220ml of water and add the dashi powder, salt, sugar and vinegar. Mix well to dissolve the salt and sugar.

Add the drained seaweed, the peppers and the chillies to the bowl. Allow to pickle in the fridge for 24 hours. Once made, this keeps for 3 days.

VEGETARIAN DASHI STOCK

MAKES ABOUT 1 LITRE

15g dried kombu
15g dried shiitake mushrooms

Place the kombu and shiitake mushrooms in a saucepan with 1.5 litres of cold water and leave to soak for 3–5 hours.

Place the pan over a medium heat and bring to the boil. Reduce the heat to a simmer and cook for about 30 minutes, or until the liquid has reduced down by about a third. Remove from the heat and leave to cool.

Strain the stock through a fine colander or colander lined with muslin to remove the scum. Squeeze out the shiitake mushrooms to get the last bit of flavoursome stock.

JAPANESE MAYONNAISE

This recipe is pretty easy to make, and a staple in the fridge for many of the dishes in this book. If you're short on time though, you can purchase some good Japanese mayonnaises in Asian supermarkets these days.

MAKES ABOUT 300ML

Whisk all the ingredients except the oil in a bowl. Begin drizzling in the oil little by little, whisking all the time until the mixture becomes thick and mayonnaise-like in consistency. This will keep for at least 2 days if stored in a clean airtight jar.

2 large egg yolks
1 teaspoon rice vinegar
1 teaspoon lemon juice
½ teaspoon sea salt
1 teaspoon sugar
200ml sunflower oil

PONZU DIPPING SAUCE

MAKES ABOUT 70ML

Combine all the ingredients in a saucepan and bring to the boil. Reduce the heat and simmer, uncovered, for 20–30 minutes or until thickened and the consistency of double cream. Use hot, warm or cold, as required.

4 tablespoons soy sauce
1 tablespoon mirin
1 teaspoon kombu dashi powder
2 tablespoons sugar
2 tablespoons lemon, lime or
   yuzu juice

TERIYAKI SAUCE

MAKES ABOUT 500ML

Combine all the ingredients in a saucepan and bring to the boil over a medium-high heat. Reduce the heat to low and simmer for 20–30 minutes, or until thickened and the consistency of double cream.

375ml soy sauce
250ml mirin
90g sugar

TONKATSU SAUCE

MAKES ABOUT 200ML

1 onion, grated
3 tablespoons soy sauce
3 tablespoons mirin
4 tablespoons tomato ketchup
2 tablespoons Worcestershire
   sauce
1 teaspoon Dijon mustard
3 tablespoons red wine

Mix all the ingredients in a saucepan with 3 tablespoons of water. Place over a medium-high heat and bring to the boil. Reduce the heat to low and simmer for about 20 minutes or until thickened to the consistency of barbecue sauce.

PLAIN RICE

This is my method for cooking plain rice. Alternatively, you can use a rice cooker. The quantities of rice and water, and their preparation, are exactly the same.

MAKES ABOUT 950G
COOKED RICE – ENOUGH
TO SERVE AT LEAST
9 PEOPLE

480g short-grain rice
720ml water

Wash the rice thoroughly in cold water and repeat at least 3–4 times until the water runs almost clear. At first it will appear murky and white from the starch. You're looking to rinse off as much of the starch as possible. Place the drained rice together with the cold water in a heavy-based saucepan and leave to soak for at least 30 minutes.

Place the pan over a high heat and cover with a lid (ideally, use a lid with a tiny hole in the top so that steam can escape alternatively wrap the lid in a tea towel). Bring to boil, then reduce the heat to the lowest setting and simmer for 13–16 minutes, or until the water is absorbed. Do not be tempted to keep lifting the lid to check if the rice is cooked – the steaming process is crucial to cooking perfect rice.

Remove from the heat then allow the rice to stand for a further 15 minutes with the lid tightly closed.

TAMAGOYAKI
JAPANESE SWEET OMELETTE

This is a versatile omelette, and often used for sushi recipes or as a side dish. You can also add various vegetables to the omelette to make it a bigger dish; just fry a selection of vegetables and then add to the egg mix before cooking.

SERVES 4

Mix all the ingredients in a large jug and stir well.

Heat an omelette pan over a medium heat. Dip kitchen paper in a little vegetable or sunflower oil and wipe the pan to grease it or drizzle a little oil into the pan, tilting the pan to spread the oil evenly.

Pour in about 15 per cent of the egg mixture. Tilt the pan to coat the base evenly with the egg mixture. When the egg starts to set, roll it up towards you using chopsticks or a spatula. Make sure you roll it while the surface of the egg is still wet otherwise the omelette won't stick.

Keeping the rolled omelette in the pan, push it back to the furthest side from you. Grease the empty part of the pan again and pour another 10 per cent of the egg mixture into the pan at the empty side. Lift up the first roll with chopsticks, and let the egg mixture run underneath. When it looks half set, roll the omelette around the first roll to make a single roll with several layers.

Repeat this process, making more omelettes to roll around the first 2 rolls, until you have used up half of the egg mixture. You will end up with 2 multi-layered omelette rolls. Move the omelette roll gently onto a sushi mat, place a plate on top to weigh it down and leave to stand for 10 minutes.

Slice the omelettes into 2.5cm-thick slices and garnish with grated daikon and serve with soy sauce for dipping.

sunflower or vegetable oil,
   for frying
4 eggs, beaten
1 teaspoon kombu dashi powder
1½ tablespoons mirin
2 teaspoons caster sugar
½ teaspoon soy sauce
pinch of salt

TO SERVE
grated daikon radish
soy sauce

INDEX

ACKNOWLEDGEMENTS

I'm filled with a joy and excitement about completing my third book, which showcases an abundance of vegetables with Japanese cooking techniques and flavours. Once again, I was very fortunate to have a fantastic team to work with to achieve this beautiful book.

I'd like to dedicate my greatest appreciation to my mother, who sadly passed away soon after my second book was published. It hit me hard losing someone who has supported me, loved me and taught me all about cooking and flavour throughout my life. I would not have reached where I am now without her.

To Tom and Jack, without whose love and support I would not have been able to go through last two years. Now the situation seems reversed, and they give me a great deal of support.

To my father, who recently turned 88 years old, and who makes me want to come back to my home in Kyoto more often than ever. I have so much appreciation for him; he provided everything the family needed all my life, and even now keeps a comfortable home for my visits.

Special thanks to Emily and Marie from the Absolute team who put everything together behind the scenes. I'd also like to thank my photographer Lauren and food economist/ recipe tester Elaine.

Last but not least, my dearest publisher Jon Croft who found me ten years ago and had the courage to publish my first book, which has since led to the third book. Huge thanks to him and Absolute.

Thank you, each one of you, for making this book come true.